8|21

# FOREVER FREE

# FOREVER

## A TRUE STORY OF HOPE IN THE FIGHT FOR CHILD LITERACY

# FREE

Tracy Swinton Bailey, PhD

OTHER PRESS
NEW YORK

Production editor: Yvonne E. Cárdenas
Text designer: Jennifer Daddio / Bookmark Design & Media Inc.
This book was set in Goudy Old Style and Trade Gothic
by Alpha Design & Composition of Pittsfield, NH

Extracts on pages 109 and 129–30 from
*Narrative of the Life of Frederick Douglass, an American Slave*, 1845.

1 3 5 7 9 10 8 6 4 2

Library of Congress Cataloging-in-Publication Data
Names: Bailey, Tracy Swinton, author.
Title: Forever free : a true story of hope in the fight for child literacy /
Tracy Swinton Bailey.
Description: New York : Other Press, 2021.
Identifiers: LCCN 2020054791 (print) | LCCN 2020054792 (ebook) |
ISBN 9781635420807 (hardcover) | ISBN 9781635420814 (ebook)
Subjects: LCSH: Literacy—Social aspects—United States. | Freedom
Readers (Program) | Literacy programs—Southern States. |
Children with social disabilities—Education—Southern States.
Classification: LCC LC152.S6 B35 2021 (print) | LCC LC152.S6 (ebook) |
DDC 379.2/4—dc23
LC record available at https://lccn.loc.gov/2020054791
LC ebook record available at https://lccn.loc.gov/2020054792

*"If there is no struggle, there is no progress."*

—FREDERICK DOUGLASS

My mother likes to tell the story of the day I was born. She tells me and whoever else will listen that I was just four pounds, so small that I could fit in the palm of my daddy's hand. From the start, though, my sound and my size did not match up.

When I came along, the seventh of seven children, my mother had been working in the hospital cafeteria for years. Many of the nurses on the maternity ward were friends, so they gave her a heads-up about her new bundle of joy:

"If you go down to the nursery and look for her, don't get scared. There's nothing wrong, we just had to move her to the back corner of the room. You see, as soon as we get all the other babies settled and sleeping, she starts hollering and wakes them up. She's about the tiniest and the noisiest thing we have had in here in a long time."

This is when my mother gets a twinkle in her eye and delivers her punch line with a smile, "She's not four pounds anymore, but she is surely still noisy."

Whenever she tells that story to a group of strangers after I've given a public talk, or she's read something I've written, I just put an arm around her shoulder and explain that I always had a lot to say.

Though I can't fathom what I could have been trying to communicate to the babies in the hospital nursery, I can definitely identify with the feeling of wanting to be heard, struggling to raise my voice in a world where people like me are expected to be quiet. All my life I've been trying to figure out why the world wouldn't want to hear me or receive me with open arms the way my daddy always did on Sunday mornings, when I was dressed for church and my hair was pressed into shiny curls. I grew up knowing that there was something of value pulsing through my veins. My parents constantly urged me to raise my voice, whether it was through making speeches at my church or singing in the choir with the other kids whose parents pushed them to learn what it meant to stand in the spotlight, to be heard.

I have wanted to tell stories, to tell my story, from the time I was in elementary school scribbling them down on half sheets of paper and sharing them with my friends on the school bus.

Yet I was constantly aware of the forces that wanted to silence me. They were heavy in the air, pushing down on me from some invisible loft, pushing in on me from every side. They were the voices of my teachers at school who carved out a time for talking and a time for listening, who valued compliance over intellect. They were the voices of the women in the community who looked at you from the corner of their eye when you chewed gum in church or laughed a little too loudly with the boys. It was the voice of my mother reminding me that I went to school to learn, not to teach the teacher: "Don't you make that school have to call me on my job."

I have walked that tightrope all of my life, struggling to figure out how to manage the stories that take shape behind my eyes in the black of the night, just before sleep creeps in, how to learn the rules of engagement, keeping the stories safe until the time was right to let them be known. The punishment for stepping out of line would be swift and harsh. Those who loved me wanted me to understand that a voice could be the most dangerous thing for a little Black girl in the seventies to have, in a world where little Black girls were problems. Make no mistake, we didn't just cause problems. We were problems.

Our hair was a problem because it would not play by the rules on its own. It had to be ironed out with a straightening comb, heated to degrees hotter than the sun, and pulled through quickly on a Saturday afternoon so it could be presentable for Sunday school. "Hold your ears," you'd be told by your mama or your auntie or your big sister when she was ready to pull out the shortest hairs on the edges, the ones most tightly curled and most defiant. "Hold your ears down," they'd warn, and then they'd touch the back of your hand with the hot comb and you'd flinch.

We spent a lot of our time flinching, recoiling from words that would slice us and eyes that burned into us, while all we wanted was to just be who we were, little girls who loved marbles and jacks and double Dutch. Just little girls with dreams and beads that made clacking sounds at the ends of our cornrows when we walked. We wanted to be able to wear our T-shirts and short pants in the summer heat and run with abandon toward the ocean waves without wondering who was watching us and thinking we were "fast" simply because our bodies had curves and developed into the thickness passed down to us through generations. In my case, I tried to become smaller, quieter, so as not to be a problem. There were those in my circle brave enough to turn up the volume on their identities in resistance. They knew that their problem status would never be reassigned, so they fought it with their fists and with their voices, and they earned a certain kind of freedom outside the lines.

Like so many before me, I've always wanted to have it both ways. I've wanted to satisfy the world's expectations while maintaining my voice and telling my story, but I have had to learn that one will always feed on the other. To have a voice is to be unique, to be shaped only by the will and determination to get the story out, to name your own reality and speak up on your own behalf. Pushing against herd mentality and destroying boxes built to contain you is at the heart of being fully human, of being free.

Out of that struggle and that balancing act, a new way of teaching, learning, and being together was formed. The Freedom Readers after school and summer literacy program, which has offered one-to-one tutoring for children living in low-income areas since 2010, is my attempt to provide a space where children can walk in the knowledge that they are not problems and that their voices matter. Young girls can find their image in the pages of a book, wild hair and all, and love her. Young boys can stand before a group and articulate hopes and dreams. Stories can be read, and aspirations can be safeguarded.

My mother was right about me from the day that I was born. I am still making noise, and I expect that the noisiness of my first day will also define my last. Because there is more to say on behalf of the children who will someday rule the world. There are more spaces to create where they are being heralded for their assets and not derided for their natural beauty. And I am not alone. As I was on my first day, I'm raising my voice to wake up everybody around me. Makes me wanna holler the way I did in the hospital nursery. It's dangerous to sit back and watch children's stories and their lights get snuffed out. This is why so many of us who love children are finding our own voices and reshaping the winds of change. Our stories are being told and retold, elevated to their proper places and received by the only ones who ever mattered, us. We are welcoming our own selves home.

# CHAPTER ONE

Books have always been some of my most powerful and influential teachers. From the times my father found the energy to read to me after having worked long hours at the stainless-steel plant to the Wednesday nights my mother took me with her to Bible study in a little abandoned building that used to be a store where I bought Jolly Ranchers and Atomic Fireballs, words were wrapped around my shoulders like a patchwork quilt. They were a river of ideas and sounds on which I floated and into which I trailed my fingers. Losing myself within them gave me the freedom to stare into a distant, cloudless sky and dream.

Like everything else I needed when I was a young child, my parents provided me with books, but I have no recollection of where they came from. I remember being surrounded by them at an early age. Maybe they had a subscription to a children's book club or perhaps they picked them up from the store when they went shopping. Whatever the case, books were a big part of my childhood, and on many nights, I would brush my teeth, change into my nightgown, and slide under the covers to wait for Daddy to read with me, before we kneeled next to the bed to pray. My favorite book was *The Monster at the End of This Book*, the story of Grover, the furry, blue Sesame Street character, who kept warning us to stop turning pages, because of the monster he knew was waiting at the end. He tied ropes to the pages so we wouldn't turn them. He built brick walls so we couldn't reach the end. When we finally arrived at the end of the book, we (the readers and Grover himself) discovered that the monster was just him. That book made me laugh so hard I almost fell out of the bed every time I heard it. After we said prayers, and Daddy kissed my forehead and walked out of my bedroom, I'd open the book next to my Donald Duck night-light and look at the pictures until my eyes burned with sleep.

In addition to Grover, I fell in love with the Berenstain Bears and Dr. Seuss and a host of other colorful books with words that rhymed. I'd go on to discover *The Boxcar Children* and *Ramona the Pest* when I was in elementary school. By the time I reached middle school I had found Judy Blume and devoured every book she'd ever written. My sister Evelyn was a voracious reader and would let me borrow books from her well-stocked shelves, which contained a few Harlequin Romances and the entire *Flowers in the Attic* series by V. C. Andrews.

In high school I dragged myself toward the summer reading list I needed to complete to be ready for my advanced English classes in the fall. At that stage in my development, I preferred books that mirrored my reality, and I didn't think my teachers would include anything that would interest me. To my surprise, I couldn't get enough of *Wuthering Heights* and *Tess of the d'Urbervilles*. *Watership Down* captured my imagination in a way I didn't expect. They weren't mirrors, but windows into another world, the temporary escape from real life that I needed. Then one summer, I took a long look at the choices on the list and chose Richard Wright's *Native Son*, which introduced me to what some young Black boys in the city faced. It raised questions of racial inequality and economic despair. I can still remember Bigger Thomas's fear rising from the pages of that paperback like smoke. With that book in my hand, I was completely at Wright's mercy, and my love for reading was solidified.

These mentors, these books of mine, spoke in no uncertain terms about the value system that should guide a life worth living. From an early age, my moral compass was set toward considering the most vulnerable members of the community. Through a confluence of situations and explicit instruction, I internalized a lesson that would shape my entire life: how we treat those with the least power and influence will ultimately define us. My mentors, on the page and in real life, fervently taught that at the end of the day, it is not about protecting the rich and the elite or positioning them to gather more wealth. It is the opposite end of the income spectrum that needs our attention most. Turning our backs on the poor is not only callous but foolish, since we are all inextricably tied to one another as citizens of one nation, one planet. No man is an island, and the quality of life experienced by the poor is not so much a referendum on their lack of ambition as an indictment of the privileged and the comfortable.

**I grew up** in North Santee, a small community in South Carolina that sits next to the Santee River and straddles Georgetown and Charleston counties. Our churches rested at the center of the community, with Singleton AME on Highway 17 and Mt. Zion AME on Powell Road. By the time I was born, four generations of my family had been a part of Mt. Zion. The preachers were like family, and just about every adult I knew consistently volunteered there to keep it running smoothly. They were stewards and trustees and secretaries and sextons and class leaders. Every person in that church knew my family. We were close-knit.

When I was a child, we were taught that we were the legacy of Richard Allen, who started the African Methodist Episcopal Church in 1816 so that Blacks could worship without the threat of racial discrimination and oppression, in a place where people who looked like us could begin to understand our intrinsic worth and God-given rights. We celebrated the ideals of our founder, who hid escaped slaves in the basement of his church and established Sabbath schools to teach literacy and elevate the status of the Black community nationwide.

It is the Black church—with its deep roots in dignity, resistance, uplift, and solidarity, that would give rise to the likes of Frederick Douglass and Martin Luther King Jr.—that has shaped me. This is where my parents walked out an intrinsic compulsion to care for their community and why they thought it was so important for me to do the same. It is within these sacred walls that I first encountered the idea of charity, depicted in Scripture as the highest form of love, the unselfish love of one's fellow man, the foundation and root of all other virtues.

My ability to articulate my understanding of charity came into focus by degrees rather than in a blinding flash of revelation. This ideology began to crystallize for me when I was a thirty-seven-year-old graduate student driving back and forth from my home in Myrtle Beach to the campus of the University of South Carolina in Columbia. I listened to books on the drive to keep my mind occupied, and one sparked a deep internal debate. Tracy Kidder's *Mountains Beyond Mountains: The Quest of Dr. Paul Farmer, A Man Who Would Cure the World* prompted questions with which I would grapple for years. What is the true meaning of charity? Is charity always beneficial, or can the purity of charity be co-opted by those who would do harm to the poor?

I've come to understand that there is a strong distinction between what we have referred to as charity in America and what I've come to call radical care. Bryan Stevenson, a social justice activist and founder of the Equal Justice Initiative, puts it this way: "We are all broken by something. We have all hurt someone and have been hurt. We all share the condition of brokenness even if our brokenness is not equivalent." Radical care can only manifest when our desire to extend charity rises out of our unique brokenness, instead of our guilt or our superiority. When we embrace radical care, we increase our capacity for compassion, and our inner strength shines through.

In addition to getting a firm grasp on concepts like charity, my reading journey has led to a struggle to understand issues of race, class, gender, and privilege. When encountering biblical passages that direct believers to be kind to the poor and needy, I have wondered who exactly well-intentioned Americans propose to help when they read about these "poor." It's more than just theory to me, it's personal. In the minds of some, my identity as a Black woman who grew up in the rural South automatically makes me a part of the group that needs to be helped. After all, when we think of riding in on a white horse and playing the role of savior, we don't see the individual faces or hear the specific names or consider the unique stories of those we are helping. Often, our imaginations are guided by what the Nigerian writer Chimamanda Ngozi Adichie has termed "the single story," a prevailing narrative about a group or culture or country that ignores the complexity of the individual.

My very existence and the work to which I have been dedicated obfuscate the image of what helpers should look like. My father walked away from formal schooling at the end of the eighth grade because there was no bus to take Black children into town to attend school, and my mother took a break from school after giving birth for the first time at age fourteen. I am the youngest of seven siblings, who grew up on dirt roads and have received some financial assistance from the government, even though both of my parents worked. I qualified for free lunch from kindergarten through twelfth grade. I am the poor that many privileged people call to mind when they try to imagine ways that they can atone for the sins of their slaveholding ancestors. I'm the product of women who scrubbed toilets and rocked white women's babies and had to catch rides on rickety buses to make less than two dollars a week. By all accounts, I should be the one needing the help.

In contrast to how they saw me, though, I never used the word "poor" to describe myself or my family members when I was growing up. I was aware that there were people who lived a tougher life than ours. Some didn't have indoor plumbing, while I never knew a time when we didn't. And I'll never forget the day we were able to trade in our box fans for central air-conditioning. We were still poor by some standards, but we were not so different from everyone else around us; proud, not looking for handouts, and unwilling to accept anyone's charity. I came from a home where education, hard work, and integrity were valued. I played jacks and marbles with my cousins on dirt roads and sang in choirs and went on church-sponsored trips. We were simply human and experienced a full range of human emotions.

As a child, I never gave much thought to the stereotypes that defined the way white America thought of us, but I realize now how much of my rearing was designed to prove them wrong. Many in our community subscribed to what the Harvard professor Evelyn Brooks Higginbotham called respectability politics, the belief that conforming to mainstream standards of appearance or behavior will protect a marginalized group from systemic injustice. We were taught to carry ourselves in a way that reflected brilliance by bringing home good grades. We had to prove that we had home training by saying "yes, ma'am" and "no, ma'am." If we wore creases in our designer jeans so sharp they'd cut your finger, expelled the kinks from our hair, and spoke with just the right amount of European lilt, maybe "they" would recognize our worth, see that we weren't so different after all. We were taught that conforming was the best way to survive and get ahead in a nation that punished individuality and demanded assimilation. If only bigotry could be solved with a school uniform. If only books could make babies bulletproof.

It wasn't until I began my graduate studies that I repeatedly encountered the terms "poor people," "low-income communities," and "underprivileged, at-risk youth" in the readings my professors assigned. As I read books and articles by Richard L. Allington like *What Really Matters for Struggling Readers* and Jonathan Kozol's *Savage Inequalities*, I began to better understand my place in America's story and how poor people were situated in the context of public education. It seemed strange to me that those labels were even necessary. In my experience, people are just people trying to navigate an environment that can sometimes be hostile and sometimes flooded with joy. I knew that there were alcoholics and drug dealers in the Black community, just as there were in the white community. There were poor people of every race making decisions that were not exactly laudable but were absolutely necessary for survival. What educators described in terms of "the other" I simply thought of as real life. It made me uncomfortable to label people who looked like me, but I also understood the language of the privileged, whose support I needed to help address the inequities in my own communities. I had to talk like them to gain their trust, to sacrifice my comfort for theirs. This became apparent in graduate school, but only became more necessary as I began to develop a grassroots nonprofit. Of all the trade-offs I had to make to survive, this may have been the most difficult. Centering white people's communication style and perspective is a constant betrayal of my own. It pierces the soul, causing the kind of pain that simmers and, in time, either collapses into itself as exhaustion or bubbles over as rage.

A lot of what led to my future success could be attributed to the luck of the draw. I was blessed to grow up in a two-parent household with healthy, aspirational parents who were not drug addicts and who didn't struggle with debilitating illness or chronic unemployment. I didn't witness repeated acts of domestic violence, wasn't forced to starve. My parents surrounded me with encyclopedias and volumes of hardback reference books from Johnson Publishing, which also produced *Ebony* and *Jet* magazines each month. These books helped me embrace my Blackness and celebrate the richness of my history. Not everyone I knew enjoyed these privileges, and I realize that my circumstances were a product of God's grace. I didn't get to choose where and when I was born, or to whom or in what skin. As the direct result of these blessings, being at the right place at the right time, and a natural gift for communication, I found myself in a position to embrace philanthropy. Molded by lessons that I had been taught from the day I took my first breath, I said yes to the call to put vulnerable people first—in a radical way. Not knowing the full extent of what I was getting myself into, I made a decision that would impact every aspect of my life. This book is about what it has meant for me to walk alongside the most unprotected among us, to run into brick walls and taste the agony of defeat, to stand in solidarity with and show compassion for Black people, immigrants, anyone lacking access to the resources they need to get where they want to go. This book is about carrying the knowledge that so much more good work is possible, but also knowing that the money, power, and influence to do more for the scores of children who could use our support are just beyond my reach. This is a story of a nation that has made promises to African Americans and other people of color that have not been kept.

**The journey** I have undertaken has pushed me to become a student of history, to try to unravel the motivations of those who best understood the realities of the silenced. Walking this path has led me to design a course of my own, with a curriculum tailored to meet my unique needs and instructors that hold forth with eloquence and challenge me directly. As I sit with them, listening eagerly for the choices they made that led to their freedom, I am transported to another plane, a dimension where not only the lessons of their struggles are laid bare, but the results of their efforts are as well. I am reminded that the work in front of me is but one aspect of the adventure. Radical care is not just about what I have sacrificed, but also about why that sacrifice matters. The other half of the equation is less tangible and difficult to grasp. It's the long-term and abiding impact of that work, which won't be seen for decades. It's the eternal impact that we won't get to see until we're on the other side.

Few of my mentors bring to the table more fire and pure unmitigated ambition than a man who rose from slavery and ultimately positioned himself to elevate an entire race. Frederick Douglass was an intellectual giant and a deeply religious man. He endured the indignities and inhumanities associated with American slavery, from savage beatings to psychological warfare, yet this brutality failed to diminish his brilliance. It would have made sense if the scars of his circumstances had broken him, if they had kept him from articulating his desires clearly and pursuing his ambitions passionately, but instead the historical record reveals a man of great accomplishment, integrity, and courage. Tied up in the chronicle of his seventy-seven years is a story of struggle that gave rise to unparalleled notoriety and a life of distinguished service.

We have much to learn from Douglass today, and he continues to teach. In his 1845 autobiography *Narrative of the Life of Frederick Douglass*, he paints a clear picture of all he endured while in bondage and generously offers advice on how we can advance. However, it is the description of his early education through an encounter with the wife of the plantation owner that speaks most directly to me. She opened a door for Douglass that would lead him out of slavery and into the company of great men. As a direct result of her tutelage, Douglass would become an orator, social reformer, writer, and statesman. Because she opened a book and guided him through the process of unlocking its meaning, a seismic shift occurred, a boy became a man, chains were immediately unlocked, and the power of human potential took flight.

None of this was lost on Douglass. His writings on literacy and its liberating power leave no doubt that he was acutely aware of the transformation taking place in his own spirit. From the moment the marks on the page were translated to word pictures in his mind, the very act of reading allowed Douglass to see himself and the world in a vastly different light. As an enslaved man, he lived a kind of hell impossible to fully conceptualize today, yet his core humanity was illuminated and unshackled instantly by words and his power to read them. "Knowledge unfits a child to be a slave," he wrote of his awakening, echoing a sentiment he remembered Hugh Auld, the plantation owner, uttering when he forbade his wife Sophia from continuing to teach young Frederick. A switch was flipped that day, a connection to a power source was activated. Douglass knew beyond question that the change was irreversible. He was forever free.

One hundred twenty-five years after Douglass's death, his abolitionist agenda is still relevant, his voice still cries in the wilderness for all those who would listen. The hills and valleys of a life's journey are not so different today from Douglass's era. Although he lived to see slavery abolished, there were mountains waiting beyond that mountain. The Emancipation Proclamation was issued by Abraham Lincoln in September 1862. Yet despite witnessing the opening of that door, Douglass also witnessed the bloody ripping apart of this nation during the Civil War and the assassination of a president. He saw Jim Crow laws rise up to take the place of the plantation system. He felt the pain of our country's darker brothers, sisters, and children lynched publicly and arbitrarily, followed by silence on the part of the courts. I can imagine that there must have been days when Douglass felt that justice would forever lie just beyond the grasp of those who looked like him.

Somehow, though, Douglass pressed on, calling attention to the racial inequality sewn into the fabric of American life until he breathed his last. And he continues to press, continues to call on us to recognize that the road ahead is long, but the work is not impossible. Our generation has witnessed the election of an African American president. Would our enslaved ancestors have dared dream it? Yet the horrific stories of African Americans shot by police and vigilante citizens publicly, arbitrarily, and sometimes with impunity still haunt us and make us question whether we've made any progress at all. The murder of George Floyd in Minneapolis on Memorial

Day 2020 led to protests in every state in America and many countries around the world. The struggle continues, and people of all backgrounds continue to respond. Unlike the case of the fourteen-year-old Emmet Till, who was lynched in Mississippi in 1955, and unlike the police shooting of twelve-year-old Tamir Rice in 2014, the images of George Floyd's murder flooded our homes in the middle of a lockdown. Floyd's death came on the heels of the deaths of Ahmaud Arbery, who was shot while going for a run through a white neighborhood, and Breonna Taylor, who was asleep at home when plainclothes officers broke down her door and murdered her. These crimes happened under the shadow of an American president who responded to a violent white nationalist rally in 2017 in Charlottesville, Virginia, where a counterprotestor was murdered, by saying, "...you...had people who were very fine people on both sides." After all of this, and in the middle of the COVID-19 pandemic, the world sat still and watched George Floyd die, and a level of righteous indignation and long-overdue moral clarity, the likes of which the world has never seen, were unleashed.

Studying Douglass highlights the fact that the mistreatment of African Americans is a part of a capitalist system designed to protect the wealth of the powerful and elite while ignoring the plight of the marginalized. Radical care requires the abolition of a racist American system that values profits over people. Police brutality is a manifestation of this system, but it is far from the only one. From inadequate health care to a criminal justice system that treats Blacks more harshly, racism flows freely through the system, often unchecked and sometimes unnoticed by many. Nowhere is this more alarming than in our education system, where innocent children first taste the poison of discrimination in the form of a curriculum that demeans and devalues them, a less-adequate education in general, as well as higher rates of suspension and expulsion. Students who belong to the mainstream have historically done well in our schools, but students of color and those living in low-income communities are struggling mightily. Furthermore, our most vulnerable students are falling even further behind when it comes to the cornerstone of a good education, literacy, defined in this context as the ability to use printed and written information to function in society, to achieve one's goals, and to develop one's knowledge and potential. In 2017, African American fourth-grade students earned the second-lowest average reading score of all groups participating in the National Assessment of Educational Progress standardized test. They ranked between American Indian/Alaska Native students, who scored lowest, and Latinx, who ranked third from the bottom. Students from the highest-poverty schools scored lower than any other group except English-language learners.

Literacy meant everything to Douglass. It was how a man could control his own destiny, carve out a place for himself in the world and make his presence known. In Douglass's mind the ability to read was worth more than gold to the enslaved, because it allowed access to the riches of the mind and proved the equality of the races. More important, though, literacy allowed the enslaved access to the truth about their situation.

Without it, the plantation owner's words had full authority and the power to define the enslaved and shape their view of the world. The oppressor could convince them that their current situation was the natural order of things, and there would be no hope for liberation. The ability to write allowed the enslaved to shape the thinking of others, opening avenues of influence and opportunity. Though Douglass celebrated the freedom that literacy brought him, he also understood the pain of coming to realize that life could be different were it not for the cruelty of your oppressors. The more he learned about the injustices and inhumanity of the institution of slavery, the angrier he became, the more despair darkened his mind. Knowledge drove him to escape his chains and eventually deliver hundreds of impassioned speeches about why the abolition of slavery was critical to the life and health of our nation.

**What Douglass held** in such high esteem is an area of crisis for our country today, where about forty-three million adults are functionally illiterate and two-thirds of fourth graders read below grade level. The National Center for Education Statistics reports that on high school graduation day, two-thirds of the students who walk across the stage continue to read below grade level. Literacy still matters today as much as or even more than it did in Douglass's lifetime. Reading is by all means still a tool of liberation for people of color. It significantly impacts health care, employment, poverty, and crime. Low reading rates lead to disparities in all of these areas, as the global pandemic exposed. For decades taxpayers have been picking up the cost of this country's failure to make good on its debt to children of color. When a patient is unable to read and understand the instructions provided by his doctor or with his medications, he is less likely to follow orders, which leads to lower rates of recovery. According to a report called *Low Health Literacy: Implications for National Health Policy*, every year we spend as much as $238 billion in health care costs as a direct result of low literacy.

When it comes to prisons, the economic impact of low literacy is even more alarming. Researchers at the Vera Institute for Justice found that in 2015, the average amount spent on each inmate in South Carolina was $20,053. In contrast, the state spent an average of $10,249 per year to educate a child in 2016. In truth, our country will either pay to adequately educate its children when they are young or pay for lower productivity levels in the labor force and higher incarceration rates when they are older. Seventy-five percent of all prison inmates struggle with literacy or did not finish high school, according to the Department of Justice. As the saying goes, "It is easier to build strong children than to repair broken men."

The work of building strong children is not easy, and has been undervalued for decades. Historically, there has been a lack of political will to address the less-than-adequate education of children of color, resulting in underfunded schools staffed by underpaid teachers stuck in a cycle of underperformance. When I was first confronted with these statistics, I realized that something different had to happen, something unconventional. Someone was going to have to step up and challenge the status quo. I didn't want it to be me. Despite the lifelong training of my mentors, I resisted the idea of raising my voice. So let me make this point clear. This is not a story of my heroism, not by any stretch of the imagination. This is a story of putting one foot in front of the other and showing up day after day. This a story about hundreds of people—rich, poor, Black, white, immigrants, educated, powerless, ordinary—who have joined the fight to make above-grade-level reading skills accessible to every child in America.

When I started this journey, I had the subject of *Mountains Beyond Mountains*, Paul Farmer, in my left ear and Frederick Douglass in my right. Convinced that the act of reading that set Douglass free could do the same for young people today, I started a nonprofit organization with the mission of improving reading skills in low-income communities. The image of Douglass as an intellectual giant born into slavery spurred me on. I knew there were contemporary intellectual giants in low-income areas waiting for an encounter that would awaken in them a thirst for knowledge. I dared to dream that a new generation of freedom fighters could step forward and change history. The work began in 2010; I chose the name Freedom Readers to honor Douglass's example of the transformative power of reading. In addition, I hoped that the children who participated in the program would gain a wider menu of options for their lives, that they would walk out Douglass's assertion that knowledge makes a man unfit to be a slave. Achieving higher levels of literacy and stronger reading skills would help set them free to choose a variety of positive paths into adulthood.

Along with Douglass, additional mentors appeared to counsel me from the pages of history in the early days of the organization's work. As I drafted plans for the shape Freedom Readers would take, the sociologist, historian, and civil rights activist W. E. B. Du Bois was a constant companion via his groundbreaking book *The Souls of Black Folk*. Within its pages, I discovered ways to make sense of what I would encounter. One passage I found especially helpful gave me the tools I needed to begin to unravel not only the power of the written word but the layers of truth that literacy allows children of color to confront:

> It is a peculiar sensation, this double-consciousness, this sense of always looking at one's self through the eyes of others, of measuring one's soul by the tape of a world that looks on in amused contempt and pity. One ever feels his two-ness,—an American, a Negro; two souls, two thoughts, two unreconciled strivings; two warring ideals in one dark body, whose dogged strength alone keeps it from being torn asunder.

Shortly after the program began, an incident occurred that would bring these realities into sharp focus for me. I share this story ten years later realizing that it symbolizes the heartbeat of our effort. We've seen variations of this story again and again, but the bottom line remains. We are teaching young people the word so that their self-discovery and heightened self-awareness might lead to their ability to "read the world," as the Brazilian educator and philosopher Paulo Freire put it. The following story illustrates the importance of keeping books in the context of young people's lived experience.

**The Darden Terrace Community Center** sits on the corner of two relatively quiet streets. With its glass doors, bright green hedges, and a row of windows near the roof, the long redbrick building has a certain curb appeal incongruent with the tough realities many of the residents of this public housing community face daily. The five or six parking spaces out front are vacant when I pull into the lot an hour before the tutors and scholars arrive. Soon cars line the street, and people march up the ramp, settling themselves into the circle of chairs I've arranged in the center of the large room. Tutors find their seats first, leaving an empty chair next to them for their scholar.

The children are still trickling in, but I've started the meeting on time. I pause to greet each one, wondering silently why they haven't all rushed in together, as they've done in weeks past. I'm still getting to know the children, but one caramel-colored girl stands out in my mind. I'll call her Raven. I wonder why she isn't with us yet. She's always the first one to join, a wide smile on her eight-year-old face. Not wanting to interrupt the flow of the meeting, I tuck these questions into the back of my consciousness and move on with the lesson.

About fifteen minutes later, Raven walks in slowly and takes her seat. I know that something is different about her. Today there is no smile, and her shoulders are slumped. Two police officers in their uniforms, with guns on their hips, show up next. The room falls silent.

"We need to speak to Raven," they announce, looking around the room. "Which one of you kids is Raven?" All eyes are trained on the officers.

"That's me. I'm Raven." There is a maturity in her voice that wasn't there before as she stands to face them. She turns to me. "Ms. Bailey. Please excuse me. I have to go handle some business."

I later learned that Raven was one of the few witnesses to a shooting that took place in Darden Terrace earlier that day. After being taken to a separate room, she told the officer what she saw and rejoined the group as if nothing happened. But the look in her eyes never left me. Ten years later, I can still see the disturbance beneath the veneer of normalcy, still hear the matter-of-factness in her voice. Raven was simply living her life and taking on responsibilities no eight-year-old should have to shoulder.

**Children like Raven,** who live in our nation's low-income communities today, are the quintessential illustration of Du Bois's concept of double consciousness. On one level, they face the realities of their situations—the trauma, the domestic violence, the lack of resources—sometimes with wisdom beyond their

years, sometimes by acting out, but the impact lurks just beneath the surface. They show up for their younger siblings, witness gang activity, find joy in their music and their friends, yet
they are not unaware of the piercing gaze of the outside world.
As a part of the Freedom Readers after school and summer
literacy program, the original group of children came together
in spaces created and reserved for them inside the communities
where they lived and celebrated their personal strengths. Today's groups tell us that they want to master public speaking, so
they stand at the front of the room each week and project their
voices, make eye contact, and speak with enthusiasm. They
think through the best way to choose books that they will
enjoy, increase their comprehension skills, and grow their personal vocabularies. These children encourage and praise one
another when they come up with unique and well-articulated
ideas, stimulated by the books that surround them and travel
home with them. Books that serve as portals into new lands
and new experiences.

Despite the laughter and the camaraderie that characterize
our meetings, the shadow of some of their school experiences
looms large. Over the years, many children have said to me,
"I can't read a chapter book. Those books are way too hard
for me." I can see their faces in my mind, young boys and girls
with limitless potential and energy to match, who have been
assigned to special education classes because they responded
to a teacher's directions with defiance one time too many. As
a result, their days are spent in self-contained special education
classrooms where the work does little to challenge them. In

these instances, the degree of academic benefit for the individual student plummets, but the mainstream classroom teacher is disrupted less frequently. The twenty-five students left in the regular classroom theoretically have a greater chance at success. But what about the one who is sent away? Granted, there are many students who are rightly assigned to special education classes due to the nature of their cognitive abilities. However, I have personally worked with students whose literacy skills were advanced and who responded well to the use of behavioral modification strategies as administered by university education professors. What many parents don't realize until it's too late is that too many of those young boys and girls in elementary school have been set on a track that will end in a certificate of attendance instead of a high school diploma. It's difficult to blame a young person who rejects such an indignity by leaving school altogether. When our splintered attention swings in their direction, society screams in unison over the dropout rate for children of color. Mothers who have sacrificed to see their sons and daughters succeed hang their heads in shame when they end up at the prison door. A disproportionate percentage of the students sent away are students of color or students who live in low-income communities.

**In response to anecdotes** like these, I believe that Douglass would point once again to the undeniable power of learning to read and to more deeply reflect on one's own situation. Some might argue that Douglass was rare in his brilliance and intellect. They might suggest that most students today are not cut from the same cloth as Douglass. But what if the cloth is not the thing that has changed? What if it is our way of teaching and reaching the students that is failing? Douglass had an encounter with a reader—one reader who made him her apprentice—who worked with him until he had gained enough competence and confidence to expand his reading horizons on his own. Conversely, we assign as many as thirty five- and six-year-olds to a classroom where they are to be taught basic literacy skills by one teacher and one assistant. Most grasp the mechanics of the act of reading, but few are affected by its magic. When our efforts do not yield the results we expected for students who enter the classroom weighed down by the burdens of poverty and toxic stress, we blame the child and their family, especially if the student in question happens to be African American. Though much has changed in the one hundred twenty-five years since Douglass's death, racial inequality is still alive and well in our society and in our classrooms.

In the wake of Douglass's writings, African American scholars have delved deeply into the notion that excellence in education is a key factor in obtaining economic freedom for marginalized groups—which in the United States means any group that is culturally, linguistically, or economically different from the dominant group. The researcher and educator Dr. Carter G. Woodson summed it up this way: "In the long run, there is not much discrimination against superior talent."

This book explores what it means to be the student who is sent away from the classroom into a restrictive learning environment, the student who has witnessed a shooting in her neighborhood, or the student who has yet to experience the magic of reading. What strategies exist to make the playing field level for them and their families? How can we make critical thinking, self-discipline, curiosity, leadership, motivation, responsibility for learning, and school literacy skills a part of our national conversation about equity and justice?

A large part of the solution lies with the willingness of our nation to recognize and assume responsibility for the dark corners of our education system and then take steps to shine a light on them. We must be careful, deliberate, and thoughtful in our efforts so as not to repeat the mistakes that have been made in the past. We must take great pains not to allow our motivations and intentions to be tainted by guilt, shame, blame, or pity. These efforts, though seemingly noble, ultimately end up perpetuating the very cycles of inequality they seek to ameliorate. But there is a better way.

Numerous programs are being implemented around the country to see how to improve children's low reading skills. I developed one such program, Freedom Readers, and offer it in the pages that follow as a way forward. This approach to strengthening communities and the educational prospects of all children invites those who have had the benefit of a good education into low-income areas for the purpose of growing literacy skills together. The program's model makes it possible for partnerships between scholars and tutors to flourish, making the time spent together meaningful for everyone involved. As a part of a community development strategy, this approach has the potential to target children's needs, giving them a chance to gain the academic and soft skills necessary for success. I've seen it work here in rural southern communities, and I'm convinced that it can work around the country. Not only do the children and their families find it beneficial, but tutors benefit from a more complete understanding of the struggles these families face. Side by side, the tutor and scholar create a new context for learning, one that challenges the need for a double consciousness and centers the unique and extraordinary story of every single child.

# CHAPTER TWO

I was an emotional wreck the day I went public with my intention to pursue a PhD. I had just graduated from Coastal Carolina University with a master's degree in secondary education. It had taken me twelve years to earn that degree, from start to finish. The twists and turns of life had led me away from the classroom, where I had taught high school English for six years, into full-time motherhood, and back into the education field as a consultant. My husband conspired with family members and friends to throw me a surprise party to celebrate my accomplishment. I had told him I just wanted to fly under the radar for once, just wanted to move on to the next challenge without much fanfare. He had other ideas.

When we showed up at my favorite restaurant, the room was filled with smiling faces. My friends and family members embraced me, gave me cards, congratulated me. I was happy to see them all, and a bit uncomfortable as the center of attention. Then the moment came for me to make a speech, to thank everyone for taking the time to celebrate me. I tried to tell them about my plans to continue my education, to go after my dream of earning a doctoral degree, but as I stood there surrounded by so much love, all I could do was cry. I wondered if I was making a mistake, asking the universe for too much. Through my tears, I asked everyone in the room, "What if I don't make it?" They assured me that I would, told me that I was one of the smartest people they knew. I stopped crying, but the doubt persisted. I did not know if I would achieve the goal, but it helped to know that they believed in me.

The day I finally reached the campus of the University of South Carolina, where I was interviewed for a spot in the program, I was both relieved and terrified. So much of my life had led to that moment. The professors were supportive, one even recommending a book I could listen to on my weekly drives. That was when I encountered *Mountains Beyond Mountains*. That's when I started to understand where I fit into the world and how I could make a difference.

As the story of Paul Farmer unfolded, my imagination was captivated by his decision to use the expertise he gained at Harvard Medical School to make an impact on a small village in Haiti that had been crippled by tuberculosis. His desire to take his work to people who desperately needed his skills resonated with me in a way that the prospect of dedicating my life to research and teaching at a university did not. When I learned about the semesters he spent caring for sick people and preventing others from becoming infected instead of writing papers for his professors, I was thrilled. Though Farmer missed virtually all the lectures and required class meetings, his professors gave him a pass, and the university granted him course credit after he aced his final exams. These accounts gave me hope. After so many years of sitting in desks as a student and then sitting behind one as a high school English teacher, I wanted more. I wanted a scholarship that could be coupled with action and passion and advocacy. Farmer's example turned me on to the possibilities of my own education and how I might blaze a new trail.

I gave little thought to the fact that there were major differences between my story and Farmer's. I didn't understand how deeply issues of race and gender separated us. I believed that in America all you needed was a dream and the will to see things through. I would later come to understand that the presence of structural, institutionalized racism makes the playing field uneven in ways that are difficult to discount. I'm not downplaying the basic differences in Farmer's situation and mine, either. He focused on medicine, and I worked in education, although in my mind, we both addressed critical issues. While Farmer saved lives with medical treatment, I wanted to improve the quality of life for people who lacked access to resources. But as a white man studying at an elite university, Farmer enjoyed a certain level of privilege that was not afforded to me. Where Farmer's professors saw the wisdom in supporting his work in the field and saw fit to substitute his real-life experience for classroom lectures, I would not be given the same opportunities. Where Farmer's work providing medical assistance to poor people in Haiti was supported by this network, my work in education was received less warmly. Kidder writes about the way Farmer connected with affluent donors like Tom White, who was so impressed by Farmer's idea that he took big bets on the organization he cofounded, Partners in Health, early on and flew to Haiti many times to participate in the work. As Kidder put it when describing the cast of hundreds that supported Farmer's vision, "lives of service depend on lives of support." I would echo and amplify that sentiment a million times, as I think of the people who volunteered their time to get trained as tutors and show up week after week for the Freedom Readers scholars. There have been steadfast financial contributors and vocal allies over the years, including the Cliff and Carolyn Ellis Foundation, which supports a number of youth-serving nonprofits in our area. Legendary basketball coach Cliff Ellis has been one of our biggest cheerleaders and his wife, Carolyn, has been a member of our board since day one. However, it hasn't been as easy to connect with millionaires who can make big bets and invest large sums of money so that Freedom Readers could hire talented people to advance our mission. Convincing foundations that we are worthy of a large multiyear grant has been a major struggle, yet we're making progress. After many years of working with us, a local foundation awarded us a three-year grant in 2019. It's a relief to know that our budget planning won't start at zero, that our efforts are being noticed. However, at the risk of sounding as if I'm diminishing the importance of this support or that I am not grateful for it, I must point out that my voice and our effort to improve reading skills in low-income communities has simply not been championed in the same way as Farmer's, and this particular discrepancy is not unique. Research shows that there is a strong divide between the financial support available to organizations led by people of color and those led by white men. More on that later.

At the same time that I was hearing Farmer's call to action, my professors were assigning readings about the underperformance of African American children and other children of color in our public schools, and I was trying to wrap my head around the root of the problem. This wasn't the first time I'd wrestled with these ideas, but my doctoral studies gave me a chance to concentrate on the issue with a laserlike focus. I became sure that the problem did not lie with the children themselves.

Though I had been recognized as a strong reader since my first days of school, I also remembered that the advanced reading group my first-grade teacher had assigned me to, and the Advanced Placement English and United States history classes I took in high school, included only a few Black students. We were a small band of "Black nerds," and we stuck together for the most part. This cohesiveness made the transition from one white learning space to another seem normal and safe for me.

In all those years of schooling, I can count on one hand the number of African American teachers I'd had.

As a researcher I wondered how my own experience seemed to be different from the prevailing narrative about African American children in today's schools. When I approached the question of why some of the children I'd observed in my own classroom and classrooms around the country seemed unengaged and unenthusiastic about school, I knew that a lack of intellectual ability was not the primary cause in many cases. I taught high school in Myrtle Beach, South Carolina, where the population was highly transient. About 1,600 students roamed the halls of Socastee High School when I taught there, most of them white. The lower-level classes that I taught, designed for students who had not done well on standardized reading tests, were majority Black. When I realized that a number of those classes ended up on my schedule because "no one else could handle those kids," I questioned my department chair about it.

"Shouldn't the kids with the most needs be assigned the most experienced and effective teachers? I'm only in my first year. There are so many teachers here who know more about pedagogy than I do. Why do they get to choose the classes that they want to teach and always end up picking the ones with the most high-achieving students?"

"Because that's the way we do things. Smart kids need to be pushed and challenged. Not all teachers can do that. You have a special gift for discipline. That's your strength. When you tell those kids to do something, they listen to you. They need a teacher who has great classroom management skills." I didn't spend much more time arguing with her, because I knew that she wasn't going to admit the truth. Some of those white teachers were more comfortable with white, affluent students who earned good grades and followed their directions. It made them feel accomplished when those children, from homes where their parents had been reading to them and building their social capital since they were in the crib, made the honor roll and got accepted to Ivy League schools. Black teachers and teachers who were fresh out of college were assigned to teach some of the students of color who did not respond to the district-mandated curriculum in the same way. After voicing my opinion a few times, I was given honors and Pre–International Baccalaureate classes to teach during my third year. The classes comprised mostly white, middle-class students.

The truth is, teaching high school classes filled with kids who have not been motivated to love reading over the years is exhausting, frustrating, maddening, and the most important role for a teacher. The students who need us most are the ones we need to be fighting for, but the department chairs and principals who determined our teaching schedules caved in to pressure and gave the most powerful teachers an easy ride, instead of focusing their energy and resources on spreading those students out or finding better ways to educate them.

From my own teaching experience, I could easily call on dozens of examples to refute the idea that most students of color underperformed. Many simply found themselves in classes where it was expected that they wouldn't engage with teachers, who for their part lacked the desire or the expertise to connect with them on a meaningful level. My teaching experiences taught me that many teachers had not spent time in the communities where students of color lived and had a limited understanding of the resources that existed there. I reasoned that if the problem did not lie with the children, there had to be an issue elsewhere. I decided to investigate the education system itself.

It became clear to me that the answers to my questions would be nuanced, a combination of multiple factors, including the validity of the criteria used to assign students to various levels or tracks, as well as the validity of mandatory standardized tests. I worked hard to distill the problem down to its most basic components by asking the types of questions that would lay bare inequities that may have gone unexamined. My initial and informal research questions included these:

- If this phenomenon could not be credited to the actual intellectual ability of the students, then did the school deliberately assign students to certain classes based on race?
- Were white children from upper-class families sent to the most rigorous classes and poor Black and brown children sent to special education on purpose?

I didn't want to consider that the answer to my questions was straightforward and glaringly unjust. No one could dispute the existence of racism in society at large, but I had discovered that racism was also at work in our education system. I realize now that my conclusions merely validated what decades of researchers before me had already shown, but coming to the realization for myself was jarring, to say the least.

During the time that my parents went to school, there was little question that whites were given preferential treatment in the educational realm. White school facilities were larger, better-equipped, and newer. School boards spent more money on the education of white students. In some areas of South Carolina where I grew up, when my parents came through in the mid-1940s, Black children had only recently been allowed to attend public school. In some towns, members of the community pitched in to make this possible by transporting students in their own vehicles or donating their time to work on the construction of the building. In other cases, schools were built with money donated through a partnership between Julius Rosenwald, a part owner of Sears, Roebuck and Company, and the famed philanthropist and educator Booker T. Washington, who became president of Tuskegee University. Black schools were underfunded, and woefully separate and unequal. After the *Brown v. Board of Education* Supreme Court decision of 1954 made school segregation illegal, Blacks began attending white schools. Many Black parents believed that the problem was solved, and that Black students would henceforth receive an education on par with what was offered to white students. A closer look would reveal that the racism that used to be so blatant simply manifested itself in educational policies, where it was harder to identify and address. Could the fact that there are more white students in advanced classes today be a demonstration of this underground and un-challenged injustice?

These questions and others circled my mind as I drove back and forth to school from Myrtle Beach to Columbia several times a week to take part in intellectual debates with fellow students and hear my professors lecture about issues of diversity, equity, and inclusion. The almost three-hour drive to campus was grueling. Most of my classes began after 4:00 p.m. so that teachers could finish their workday and still arrive on time; this frustrated me since I was not teaching. A late start meant a late finish, and I wouldn't arrive home until close to mid-night. I relished my studies, though. I was being challenged, and my thinking was being reshaped in powerful ways. For the most part, I threw myself into my readings and encountered in my own thinking biases that I had not known were there. For example, I took a class focused on multiculturalism and diversity that delved deeply into the politics of difference. My upbringing had prepared me to think deeply about racial dis-crimination, but when my professor talked about allyship and how heterosexual teachers had a moral obligation to create safe spaces for their gay students, she struck a nerve. I knew that what she was saying was right, but I squirmed in my seat for the rest of the class. It was her prompting and the video she shared of young gay people telling their stories that caused me to think deeply about an uncomfortable truth. If I was going to claim to embrace inclusion and equity, I had to speak out on behalf of any group that was being mistreated, just the way

I expected whites to be allies of people of color. I remember exactly where I was sitting in the classroom when that professor's lecture called me out without even knowing it. My grades reflected my commitment to the assignments, but my life was beginning to reflect my commitment to personal growth.

That experience reminded me of a student who took my journalism and newspaper production class during the second year that I taught at Socastee High School. I'll call him Charles. It was the late '90s in a conservative town, and he was openly gay. As the school newspaper's editor, Charles thought it was important to raise his voice in support of other gay students in the school. He wrote a column sharing how it felt to be silenced, marginalized, and mistreated by society. As the paper's adviser, I saw nothing wrong with allowing Charles to express his views, but the school administration disagreed. I was required to submit a draft of every issue to the principal for his approval about a week before it went to press each month. One afternoon I was called into the principal's conference room to find four assistant principals sitting around the table. My recollection of the exact content of Charles's column along with every detail of the meeting has gone fuzzy with time, but the overall message was clear. It went something like this: I sat at the far end, while they explained to me that I was being manipulated by Charles because I was a young teacher. They told me that his views had no place in the school newspaper, that they pushed the boundaries of decency, and that they would never see the light of day. We were not asked to revise or edit. They just killed the whole thing. I was told to start being wiser and more discerning as the school newspaper's adviser.

Instead of going to war on behalf of Charles and other gay students, I followed the directives I was given. I called a newspaper adviser at a nearby school who had won numerous state high school journalism awards and told her that I felt as if Charles's first amendment rights had been violated. Furthermore, I felt as if my leadership of the newspaper staff had been stepped on. She said that I could try to fight the school's principal, but I probably wouldn't win. So I talked to Charles, who was justifiably livid when we pulled his column from the school newspaper at the last minute. I advised the newspaper for three years, and that moment looms in my mind larger than any other.

At that point in my life I didn't know about Kimberlé Crenshaw's concept of intersectionality. I didn't realize that race, gender, class, sexuality, and other points of oppression could come together to create pressure from a number of angles, pressure that could ultimately crush a person's spirit. That class on diversity called me out for not advocating more aggressively on Charles's behalf. I certainly could have done more to protect him and his voice. I should have at least said to the five principals sitting around that conference table that Charles had just as much of a right to tell his story as they or any student at the school did. But power stepped forward to protect the status quo, and I failed to challenge it. After wrestling with my own cowardice, I vowed to do better. From that moment forward I knew I had to be more than just an ally in my heart, especially if I expected my white colleagues to do the same for me.

**The longer I worked** on my degree, the more and more clear my responsibility to my parents and to my community became. Because so much had been given to me in the way of their support, guidance, and discipline, I knew that a great deal was required from me. Once I finished my degree, I would join an elite group of African Americans. According to an article by Adam Harris published in *The Atlantic* in 2019, only 5.4 percent of the roughly 50,000 people who earned a PhD each year between 2002 and 2017 were Black. Those of us who manage to successfully navigate the maze of high cost, politics, and microaggressions find ourselves uniquely positioned to speak on behalf of Black families, who have been historically denied equity in education. I didn't know what that would ultimately look like for me, but the weight of walking through gates that had been previously locked was heavy on my shoulders. I would become one of the gatekeepers, and what I did with that power was no small consideration.

I realized that many generations of strong, determined people who came before me were not given the chances I was given, yet their wisdom was boundless. They taught through example and through their courage and their faith; those lessons were ingrained in me the way they were passed to my parents by the role models in their lives. We lived on land that had once belonged to my great-grandmother. My aunt says that my great-grandmother and her mother before her might have been enslaved on a plantation not too far from where I grew up. Hopseewee Plantation was not only the home of my ancestors, but it was also home to one of the signers of the Declaration of Independence, Thomas Lynch Jr. Like many whose ancestors bore the scars of enslavement, I do not have clear details of my heritage; however, there is no question that within me beats the heart of the ones who survived. Four hundred years of oppression didn't break my mother or her mothers. My father stood proudly in his garden and looked over his okra and collard greens with the understanding that if he did his job as a parent right, I would someday pick up the baton and reach back for those who needed a hand. Just as he would leave a bucket of butter beans on the porch of a neighbor, I was expected to give what I had to the community to make it stronger.

The lessons I learned from my parents were reinforced by the sermons I heard at my church week after week. The church I'd join as an adult was as different from the one I went to when I was growing up, Mt. Zion AME, as the sun and the moon. Where Mt. Zion had been chosen for me when I was an infant, my fiancé and I chose this church for a number of reasons. We felt as if the messages spoke directly to us. And above all, the church held racial reconciliation as one of its core values. The promise and possibility excited us. It was the first time we'd heard a southern white evangelical preacher speak openly about racism and the steps he was trying to take to kill it.

Unlike the AME Church, this evangelical church we joined was not built on the idea that African Americans needed a

place where they could worship without the threat of racial oppression, which caused a great amount of cognitive dissonance
on our part. We heard "racial equality" when what was really
being offered to us was racial togetherness, the opportunity to
sit next to a white person on a Sunday morning. These are
two very different realities, and when it finally dawned on me
that we were not even speaking the same language, I was dev-
astated. After having been brought up in a church where the
Bible was a tool of liberation from racial discrimination and a
symbol of pride and hope, we stepped into a situation where
the overwhelmingly white congregation felt uncomfortable
even talking about race. When we tried to bring up the subject
and devise a strategy for moving forward, we heard the words,
"You care about race and I care about Jesus."

Those words hit me hard because for me the implication
was clear. There was only one Jesus, and that man was obviously white and color-blind. There was no white heaven, no
Black heaven. It followed that we shouldn't acknowledge race
on earth either. That statement placed the few Blacks in the
church on one side, and the whites, who had a very different
experience with race, on the other. I was angry, because I had
been taught better. I knew better than that in the pit of my
soul, because my parents and the AME Church had taught
me better than that. But I rationalized. I thought maybe I was
being too sensitive, just like they told me I was. I tried to listen to their point of view and tried to remember that progress
would only happen if both sides kept an open heart. I spoke up
about the way I felt welcomed but invisible. I told them about

how I felt that I had to leave my culture at the door. The white people to whom I was closest told me it was a figment of my imagination. Told me I just needed to try harder, to reach out more, to stop expecting people to exclude me, to get rid of the chip on my shoulder.

More than ten years after we joined the church, and just as I was starting classes in the PhD program, the pastor started a series of sermons, "Love in Action," which focused on community outreach. He told us that the love of God was meant to be shared, not kept within the walls of the church. My heart beat a little faster every time he said it. It was like those words had been formulated exclusively to motivate me. Maybe it was possible to bring together my concern for families living in low-income communities and my passion for Scripture.

It wouldn't be long before an opportunity presented itself. One Sunday, as I sat in the red cushioned chair near the front of the cavernous auditorium, I heard an announcement inviting folks to visit one of the local public housing communities. My friend Cindy had pulled together a chapter of All Pro Dad, a national organization founded with help from NFL football coach Tony Dungy to help fathers reconnect with their children. Cindy and her husband Tysin were one of the few Black families in the church when we joined. We became friends instantly, and have had many conversations over the years about the disconnect between what our church said about race and what it ended up doing. We both tried to initiate programs and groups that would help this mostly white congregation live up to its own stated ideals. Supporting each other was what we did best. Cindy was going to be hosting a breakfast at Darden Terrace, a public housing community just a few miles down the road from the church, to do something nice for the children and parents there. Knowing that I relished every opportunity to use my classroom teacher voice, she invited me to be the guest speaker at the breakfast.

The meeting started early, around 8:00 a.m. on a Saturday. Quite a few members of the church showed up to be a part of the gathering. They brought their pots and pans, and scrambled eggs on the stove at the Darden Terrace Community Center. They brought muffins and juice and all kinds of fruit to share. Most of the members of the church were white, some middle class, others working class. I believe strongly that everyone who showed up that cold morning came with good intentions, but with a little apprehension as well. I can't say for sure what motivated them to sign on to an initiative led by one of the few Black members of the church, but I had come to know and trust many of them. For whatever reason, they showed up. And that says something. Most of the residents of Darden Terrace who showed up were young Black moms. The meeting room of the community center was animated by the sound of their children's laughter.

The thing I remember most about that meeting was the way we segregated ourselves. The adults in the room waited without saying a word while the food was being prepared and the tables set. It didn't surprise me, but it did make me a bit uncomfortable, so I moved from Cindy's group to the Darden Terrace group, introduced myself to all of the moms, and shook their hands. I was just about the only one to cross over, though. Church members stayed on one side of the room and the moms stayed on the other. Kids roamed freely without a care in the world, running, playing, having the time of their lives, completely oblivious to the awkwardness in the air. We were reinforcing the social structures that had been ingrained in us since the day we were born. Our churches were separate. Our schools embraced the philosophy of academic tracking, in which students were separated based on test scores. And even within our own somewhat racially mixed congregation there was a corner on the far right side of the church where many of the Black members sat together. We stick with what is comfortable, we seek out those who look like us. Some of the white members of that church flew Confederate flags and would deride Colin Kaepernick for taking a knee. The moms were probably thinking that we were just another group of white and want-to-be white folks looking down on them to make ourselves feel better. You could almost cut the absence of trust with a knife. But I had joined the church with the desire to see advancements in race relations take hold. I hardly ever passed up the chance to get people from different backgrounds talking. This was Cindy's show, however, and I was there to support her. I took note of the distance between groups, and immediately started to wonder if there was a way to cross this invisible ocean, to build a bridge that would make things seem less weird and foreign, create a new kind of togetherness that would not manifest naturally but would achieve the mission of the event: bringing people together.

We ate our breakfast, still on opposite sides of the room, and then I gave my short talk that morning, trying my best to keep all the different audiences engaged. I modulated my voice and made eye contact with the children especially. I called up every ounce of enthusiasm in me, and I think it was well received. The applause seemed genuine; the feedback was positive. That would be the first time I addressed a group at Darden Terrace, but it would not be the last. Not by a long shot.

I told the group what had been told to me in the AME Church and in my community. I echoed for them the positive message that had drawn us to Christ Community Church in the first place. I hoped that my words would resonate on some level with everyone in the room:

> You are special. Everything about you is special. You may not realize it. You may never let your mind wander in that direction, but you are special. Maybe nobody has told you in a while, but you are so incredibly valuable and worthy and important. There is something so unique about you that the world is a completely different place just because you are here. And each and every one of us in this room today was created for a specific purpose. This work is so tailor-made and powerful that if you don't do it, that work simply won't get done. That's why it's so urgent that you understand how much you are loved and how special you are. When you know this in your heart, then you can start to unwrap the gifts that God gave you and you can start moving

toward your destiny. Greatness is in your DNA. Time to unlock what's inside. Let's go!

**Mr. B is a heavyset Black man** who doesn't smile much, but on the rare occasion that he does show his teeth, his cheeks balloon and his eyes turn to slits. In addition to serving as programs coordinator for the Housing Authority of Conway, he was pastoring a Black Baptist church in the area when I met him. Maybe that's why his demeanor came off as a bit stern, haughty, and authoritarian. Though I knew that we were around the same age, I could hear the grizzled old preacher in his voice the day I sat across from him as he reclined behind the wide desk in his office. He'd been intrigued by the speech I gave at the breakfast and invited me to come in to speak with him about organizing an after school program for the community's children.

"These kids need something to keep them occupied after school. Too many of them are getting into mischief and they are not being properly supervised," he told me in his gravelly, booming voice. His glasses fit snuggly across his round face.

"I am sure that we can help you. I already have some ideas about what we can do," I told him, leaning forward in my chair.

"Good, good. What do you have in mind?"

"Well, I think we need something that is going to be very structured. That's what's needed. And we're going to bring in books to help these kids read better."

"Yes, that's right. You need to help them with their homework. That is something they need."

"No, I don't mean help with homework. I mean help with reading. The kids need to get their reading skills stronger so they can do better in all their classes. I used to be an English teacher, and we can share some strategies with them. Reading is the building block to success in all classes."

"Exactly! That's exactly right. I read all the time. You know I grew up in Section 8 housing myself. And without a father, either. It was books that helped me get where I am today. I understand how important they are. But you have to understand something too. These kids might show up one time, but they won't be coming back to your program after they find out you want to do something structured and focused on books. That will not work out here."

"Why not? I think it might be tough to get it established in the beginning, but the kids are smart. If we offer them something structured, they might get a whole lot out of it."

"I'm not going to stop you from trying. You won't be the first one to try and fail. Just don't say I didn't warn you."

**Mr. B and the housing authority's executive director** gave me their blessing. They promised to put the word out about what we wanted to do. Over the next weeks, I sent Mr. B emails that went unanswered and attempted to reach him by phone, to no avail. To put it mildly, the office was slow to respond to questions and requests for assistance as I tried to plan out the hours we'd meet and other logistical aspects. But I knew where the community was located and how to get to the families and kids I wanted to reach. By that time, my efforts were fueled by the belief that I was given this work to do by a higher power for a unique reason. I was on a mission. A few unanswered messages wouldn't stop me from changing the world. It's hard to describe the adrenaline rush of finally saying yes to doing something out of the box and crazy scary. Even though only a few of the dots connect, and you have no concept of the big picture, you keep making calls and showing up and doing what feels like the next right thing. To some, it looked like passion, dedication, drive, grit. Looking back on it now, I can detect elements of fanaticism, delusion, evangelical fervor, and unrealistic idealism. I can only imagine how obnoxious and tough to be around I must have come across to folks in my circle. In some small way, reflecting on that feeling helps me empathize with people who don't get excited about the same things as me but who go after their convictions with that same fire. You can see it a mile away.

My unwillingness to relent did come in handy, though. The radio personality Michael Baisden had a syndicated show on the air right around the same time that we kicked off Freedom Readers. One of Baisden's big concerns was the state of Black children in America. To raise awareness of the issues related to Black kids and promote his radio show, he launched a hundred-city tour called Save Our Youth. One nonprofit in each city would receive a $10,000 donation to help it positively impact the lives of young people.

The local radio station planned a day-long event in the exhibit hall at the convention center, with area speakers and vendors. A huge crowd was expected. We were excited to be there with organizations that had been serving the community for decades, because Freedom Readers was only a few months old. We appreciated the chance to recruit tutors and get the word out about our mission. By the middle of the day, I was starving, and my young son and daughter needed a break, so I went with a friend to pick up something to eat. I had just taken the first bite of my hamburger when my phone started blowing up. Apparently, Freedom Readers had won the $10,000 prize, and no one could find me. The third time they called for me, my husband asked Cindy Young, who had served as a team leader and was a founding member of the tutoring team, to represent me and the organization. As she described the scene later, Cindy reluctantly started walking toward the stage, where Michael Baisden stood waiting with the big check. But before she could even get halfway there, someone else had ascended the stage and claimed the big check and all the credit. With a laugh and a shake of her head, Cindy described that big, cheesy smile on Mr. B's face when he welcomed her to the stage. Fortunately, his ability to grab the spotlight in that moment did not translate into claiming the prize money. I deposited the actual check into the Freedom Readers bank account when it arrived a few months later.

**At the same time** I was chasing Mr. B and trying to get some concrete plans down on paper, I was settling into the life of a graduate student. The classes in the PhD program at the University of South Carolina continued to rock my world, causing me to rethink ideas that I had never examined until that point, pushing me to bring together what I had experienced as a student, teacher, and educational consultant with what was in front of me on the page. It was as if the research spoke to me in the night, called to mind the faces of children who sat beside me in classrooms when I was a child, as well as those who sat in front of me when I took my place at the front of the room. Memories of Marvin haunted me. He had been the skinny kid with a big Afro who sat in the far back corner of my English I class at the end of the day. No matter what novel approaches I tried, no matter how many times I stood next to his desk and taught from there, no matter how many student-teacher behavior management contracts we developed or conferences I called, Marvin would come in, put his head down, and fall into a restful slumber accentuated by light snores that rose above his desk every now and then. I tried everything I knew, but I was never able to reach that kid. I know that I failed him.

What I didn't fully grasp at the time is that I was a part of an educational system that was built on white supremacy. Inside that system, everything about Marvin and Black boys like him was suspect. The standards we teachers tried so hard to teach and the frameworks for teaching them that were adopted by our state were completely devoid of Black perspectives. Since the time these children entered kindergarten, this educational system communicated to them that they were not good enough. The way their forebearers talked was quietly derided, the textbooks ignored them, and very few of the novels I tried to get them to read had anything to do with their lived experiences. Although I worked in a beautiful building with cutting-edge technology in the late '90s, historically, underfunded schools and dilapidated facilities were nothing new to Black students. It wasn't until graduate school that I was fully able to begin to understand the big picture and the fact that I was but a small cog in a very old and very large wheel. Expecting Black students to be attentive and excited about learning without challenging an oppressive system would never get me the results I wanted.

It was in the course of learning about sociocultural theory, funds of knowledge, critical race theory, and culturally relevant teaching that I conceptualized Freedom Readers. I had been inspired by the countless studies demonstrating that there was a better way to go about reaching students than I had tried when I was in the classroom. The decision to create and implement a new program rose out of conversations with people like Mr. B, who underestimated what the children could do as well as the new ideas with which I was being confronted. More than that, though, the idea for this new way of interacting with students seems to have been rooted in the deepest caverns of my spirit since childhood, like a pearl developing in the belly of an oyster. The first glimmers of the idea made themselves known to me in 2008 and 2009, in the middle of the political possibilities of the Obama era. For the first time since South Carolina turned red in the '60s, many of us in the conservative, Republican South had started to dream again. I could see it in the faces of my parents, their siblings and their friends, a kind of radiance that I had never seen before Obama spoke on television. On the morning of the presidential election, when it was possible for them to put a Black man in the White House for the first time in their lives, lines snaked around high schools, and churches became polling stations for the day. People showed up hours early and stood in the rain. Without a doubt, I was swept up by that energy. It was nothing short of electric.

What moved me forward on the wave of that pulsing enthusiasm was understanding that without a structure, without some sort of concept on which to hang their dreams, people would quickly return to their routines and their disappointments, quietly wishing that the Hope and Change Obama had promised was real. Although I couldn't predict the outcome of Obama's eight years in power, and I'll leave it to the historians and pundits to say whether or not he was a success, I did know that in our small, rural corner of the world, we would be left to fend for ourselves when it came to hope. Campaigns pack up and move on. Dirt roads are easily traded in for the flashing lights of the city, for more liberal and racially diverse blue states, like California. Yet even after we watched the inaugural balls with stars in our eyes, seeing Michelle Obama floating across our screens dressed in her ivory one-shoulder Jason Wu design, the candles of our hope that were ignited had not gone completely out. They may have dimmed, but they still burned.

Those of us who are willing to give up a degree of comfort for the sake of our children protect the fragile flicker of hope with our lives, not because we are indefatigable or bulletproof, but because we know that our children need us to carry on the fight. They are worth fighting for. It is our moral imperative to provide safe spaces where they can learn, to protect their right to excel, to stimulate their curiosity with questions that inspire deep thought. So it was within the walls of a white evangelical church that I made the first call for warriors, the same church that had supported Cindy's All Pro Dad effort months earlier. I wasn't sure how my invitation to venture into the local housing projects on a weekly basis would be received. Surprisingly, the response was strong. My white brothers and sisters, many of whom would end up supporting Trump a few years later, and who vilified Obama for what they often said were purely political reasons, saw themselves as a part of the solution. Perhaps our ideologies did not always align, and they had not read the same studies I'd analyzed and discussed, but they came to the table wanting to know how I thought they could help.

The work that was started in one of the meeting rooms of that church continues. It has branched out from the housing authority into AME churches, schools, and community centers. It has embraced white, Latinx, and African American children. We've studied the planets, money management, and the habits of happy kids. We've held awards ceremonies where children showcase their talents to packed rooms of community members, and we've designed ways to help parents focus on their own needs so they can better support their children.

Much has changed, but the need to open avenues of hope for students has only intensified over the years. Since the beginning, we've always paired one child with one adult in order to give relationships a chance to flourish. Special bonds have been formed as a result. This aspect of weekly meetings will never fall away. In the forty-five minutes that they spend together reading and telling stories, children and adults allow themselves to be seen. The sometimes suffocating and sometimes low expectations of school can be replaced with the joys of being heard, validated, challenged, encouraged, and supported.

I would graduate from that doctoral program four years after Freedom Readers took flight. I'll never forget the way the light reflected off the hardwood floors of the Koger Center as I made my way to the middle of the stage after hearing a disembodied voice enunciate my entire government name. I turned my back, and an unknown white man placed a hood around my neck. I grinned, floating off the stage and back to my seat. My family took up an entire row near the back. My parents, my brother, who flew in from Texas, my sisters from Atlanta, my nieces and nephews, friends from college, my pastor, and a Freedom Readers board member. Everyone came to see me take that giant leap forward, and the pride that swelled up in me was almost too much to bear. I thought of lines from Maya Angelou's poem "Our Grandmothers": "I go forth / alone, but stand as ten thousand." My mothers and their mothers; my daddy's smile and the light in his eyes, and his daddy; Carter G. Woodson, W. E. B. Du Bois, and Frederick Douglass; Michelle Obama. A cloud of witnesses walked me across that stage. The scholars at Freedom Readers and the parents who made sure they showed up on time each week, and the tutors who were the thread that kept the fabric together around the thrashings of our struggle.

Few of them realized that I had almost been excluded from the celebration that day in May 2013. A few weeks earlier, everything I'd worked toward and hoped for was ripped apart in front of my eyes. Like so many children of color in our public schools, I received a rude awakening. I would soon learn that the way I saw myself did not align with the way I was being seen.

# CHAPTER THREE

When PhDs tell the story of the day they defended their dissertation, there is usually a happy ending. Some talk about the long, grueling hours they invested in research, reading books, and conducting interviews, but the conversation inevitably turns to triumph, that feeling of having run a marathon and hitting wall after wall only to finally cross the finish line with your last ounce of energy. I've completed two full marathons. The metaphor is apt. But my story is different. My story takes a turn that most do not. If we further the analogy of the marathon runner, what happened in my case is more like the athlete who reaches mile twenty-five in a 26.2-mile race, only to be pushed to the ground by some unstable onlooker who jumps out from the sidelines. Instead of being congratulated for reaching the pinnacle of my educational journey, I was told that I had failed. For reasons I struggle to fully comprehend to this day, I was allowed to graduate only after being told that I would not, and watching a lifelong dream shatter like glass.

As with all long races, this story starts long before the day I stood in front of my committee. Twelve years earlier, a defining moment prepared me for the road ahead.

**Shannon and I sat together** on the couch in her living room looking over assignments. In order to satisfy the state's diploma requirements, the school assigned a certified teacher to deliver what it termed "homebound instruction." Like clockwork, I'd show up two times a week to discuss with Shannon what her classroom teachers told me she should know and do. It helped that I had been one of her teachers before we both left the high school on maternity leave. She had been enrolled in my ninth-grade English class. A year later we sat in her living room with her son in a baby carrier next to our feet, while back at home with my husband, my son jumped in his bouncy chair.

The mobile home park where Shannon lived with her mother and two brothers wasn't far from my neighborhood. Shannon was always waiting for me, inviting me in with a warm smile. She told me that day that her mother was gone to work and that her teenage brothers would probably be coming in and out.

She always turned the television off when I arrived so that we could concentrate on the lessons I brought with me. I was jotting down questions for her math teacher when I heard a loud crash coming from the back of the trailer.

"It's just my brothers," she told me before reaching down to replace the pacifier in her son's mouth. "They're always getting into it."

It wasn't the first time I'd heard them argue. There seemed to be a constant tension between the two boys. Shannon and I tried to ignore them, doing our best to stay focused on her lessons.

The second loud noise was the older brother crashing into the wall of the living room before he slid down to the floor. In seconds, the younger teen stood over him yelling in a loud voice, threatening to kick him in the side.

"Hey! You guys cut it out. Cut it out. Can't you see me trying to get my schoolwork done?" I could tell that Shannon, now sixteen, had been in this situation before. The room felt as if it were shrinking around me as the older boy got up and charged his brother with the handle of a broom, catching him across the forearm with a blow that made a loud popping sound. The offended brother screamed, got a knife from the kitchen, and held it in his hand for a few seconds with a look in his eyes that said everything I needed to know.

By this time, the baby was screaming. Shannon was also screaming, and threatening to call her mom at work. I could feel a vein in my neck pulsing, the one that goes haywire when I get scared.

"I'm sorry, Shannon. I can't do this." I placed my notepad into my black schoolbag and headed toward the door. I asked the school to find another instructor for Shannon that day, and I looked for another job, but I never forgot that family and the issues with which they wrestled. I think about Shannon often, the way she managed her household while her mother was away, while learning to be a mother herself. The way she took control and talked her brothers down while I prepared to leave. I did not detect one trace of victimhood or even fear in the set of her shoulders or the steel of her voice. Instead, I observed determination, agency, a certainty that education would offer her the best chance at a better life. At the time, I didn't have the capacity to provide all that Shannon needed, but she inspires me every day to reach out to girls like her, to use all I've gained to light a path for them.

**Twelve years later** I sat in a book-lined room in Wardlaw Hall with the four members of my dissertation committee. I was asked to make a presentation that day on the research study that I had conducted in a low-income community, where Freedom Readers was serving children in grades kindergarten through five. I was nervous, but confident that I had listened carefully and responded to all of my professor's suggestions and guidance. I continued to listen as they detailed the weaknesses of my work. They pointed out the ways in which they thought my writing showed an unfamiliarity with life in low-income areas. They said that I didn't understand that such families had value on their own and that they didn't need me to come in and fix them. They told me that they got the sense that I didn't believe those families were good enough, that I was trying to change them fundamentally.

I had expected some pushback. No dissertation is perfect, and I'll be the first one to admit that I didn't know what I was doing. That's why I leaned on my adviser's directions so heavily. I asked her to make the expectations clear, and I believed that she had. I studied each one of those expectations as they were spelled out to me and made sure that her approval was granted. I was meticulous in this regard because the mere attempt at writing a dissertation was a monumental risk, one few people I knew personally had dared to take. So I wasn't surprised when committee members started a list of what I needed to revise. My adviser had prepared me for that part. But I didn't expect to hear that my attempt to defend my work had failed, that I would not be permitted to walk out that door on that day having earned a PhD. To be honest, what happened in that room defies logic, both in my mind and the minds of the committee members. When I reached out to the two I could find when I started working on this book seven years later, they admitted that they didn't remember the meeting, and the details the way I explained them didn't make sense at all. I couldn't agree more.

**The road that led me** to the door of the University of South Carolina was anything but conventional. I had gone from being a full-time English teacher to being a full-time at-home mom to working with children who had been assigned a home-bound teacher.

For a while after that I worked for my school district as a consultant. The superintendent arranged to have me visit two high schools each week, one on Tuesdays and another on Thursdays, to offer support for classroom teachers. That was my understanding of my role and what I believe she had com-municated to the principals of the schools. One principal set up an office for me in an old supply closet with a telephone, a table, and a desk, promising to send someone to talk to me about a classroom visitation schedule. That schedule never ma-terialized, though I pushed the school leadership to do so, and I spent most of my time at the school alone in that closet, with very little interaction with the staff. A new superintendent was hired six months into that arrangement, and the position ended as abruptly as it started.

Then I got a call from one of the former assistant principals at the high school where I taught. Angela told me that she had found a national organization that was doing consulting work for urban school districts. She thought I'd be a perfect fit for the National Urban Alliance for Effective Education (NUA) and encouraged me to apply. I dismissed the idea at first. There I was in my pajamas, reading her email telling me to fill out an application and fly to New York for an interview. It seemed so far out of my reach at the time that I almost laughed out loud. I had not yet finished my master's degree, and I only had five full years of teaching under my belt. What did I have to offer to a national organization providing assistance to teachers in the inner city? I have to give it to Angela, though. She never let up for a minute. She obviously saw something in me that I couldn't see in myself at the time. She continued to email and call me until I filled out the application and was invited to an interview with the executive team. By the time I made it over all of those hurdles, I had an idea that the leadership was interested in me, but I was still surprised. I was one of the youngest educators in a room of college professors, retired administrators, and published authors. It was thrilling and terrifying all at once.

As a consultant with the NUA—we called ourselves mentors—I was assigned to work on teams that met in a city to provide professional development in a variety of schools. My first assignment sent me to Newark, New Jersey. When it comes to educational experience, Newark was just about as far away from Myrtle Beach, South Carolina, as I could get. I honestly did not know that there were still segregated schools in America. But when I stood in the crowded halls of Barringer High School, surrounded by a sea of Black and brown faces, listening to the multiplicity of languages and dialects being spoken by students from places like Haiti and Puerto Rico and Jamaica, I knew that I was in a different world.

Working with the NUA broadened my horizons like nothing else could. Witnessing firsthand what was happening in a variety of schools in a variety of settings while in the company of smart, visionary educators who were processing the same things changed me as a teacher and as a person. The experience made me more compassionate, more aware, and much more determined to fight for educational justice.

The professional development that I facilitated as an NUA mentor focused on cultural relevance, among other things. It was this aspect of my work that gave me my first glimpses of the theories that explain the struggle inherent in being a young person of color in this country trying to get a good education. Up to that point, I had lived it, but I had never been involved in a serious scholarly discussion about the beauty and power of my own cultural heritage. Augusta Mann, one of the NUA's senior scholars, changed all of that. Every one of her presentations celebrated the identity and contributions of Black and brown people. She shared photographs of Black love that challenged the notion that most Black children came from broken homes. She shared detailed timelines of Black history that went beyond slavery and back to Africa. She taught all of us about the African principles that she drew on to create teaching strategies that would touch the spirit of young children of color. "We have a problem that need not be," she'd say in reference to the underachievement of Black students. My heart swelled every time she said it, because her words rang so true.

None of these experiences were considered by my committee, because the dissertation was not about me. My writing focused exclusively on my research, which involved two mothers and the way they created environments of excellence in their homes. In the methodology section of my paper, I described the way that the Freedom Readers program worked, because I needed to explain how I had encountered the participants in my study in the first place. At the time I did not consider myself an abolitionist teacher, but looking back I can say that there is no other definition for what I had become. Like those who sought to end slavery more than one hundred years before I was born, my intention was to abolish schools as we know them to make room for new spaces of learning that better meet the needs of children of color. The establishment of that program presented everyone involved in it with a kind of freedom that schools could never offer. The freedom to take risks and learn new things without the fear of failing the next test. The freedom to be positive and supportive and choose to incorporate play and allow scholars to dictate the direction of the learning.

Had I set out to shine a light on the program I created, I would have explained that Freedom Readers was born of a desire to create safe spaces for children living in low-income communities, spaces where they could exhale and be themselves, the way I did when I was learning about and teaching culture as an NUA mentor.

Inherent in the initial design of Freedom Readers was a respect for the voices of these children and a celebration of their identities. The first meetings took place outside of the school building. We'd find a church fellowship hall or a community center where we could distance ourselves from attempts to militarize schools by staffing them with security guards and resource officers, where there were no state standards or Eurocentric curricula, where all of the adults in the room were trained to focus their attention on one child and help that child gain not only reading skills but a sense of pride in who she is and where she comes from. The mere idea of Freedom Readers is a reimagining of what education can and should be for all children who have been pushed to the margins and viewed with suspicion by overworked, under-resourced teachers who have only a shallow understanding of what it means to be Black.

Looking back on the situation, it doesn't surprise me that my professors were invested in protecting the system to which they belonged. As members of the university faculty, they were considered experts in their field. The papers they published were read by practitioners all over the country. The presentations they gave at conferences were well attended. Although they critiqued my dissertation for being weak in wokeness, their reputations and livelihood depended on schools maintaining the status quo. As a student in that program, I did a lot of reading about power. Each of us must be willing to interrogate our own power in various situations. We have the power to open new channels of discovery, and the power to shut them down. We have the power to define for others the one right path to wokeness and the power to create room at the table. My story proves that there is more than one right way to fight oppression and be woke. Though it may have seemed most effective to my professors for me to stand up to racism by doing a better job of incorporating critical race theory into my paper, it is also effective to go into low-income communities and sit next to a child and help him decode. The two approaches need not be at war. We can respect each other's truth and support each other's tactics in the same fight. If it benefits children in the end, we can claim a collective victory.

As an evolving disruptor and educational abolitionist, I felt constrained by the straitjackets PhD candidates were forced to wear. Authority figures tell you what to read, when to read it, and how to interpret the reading. A diversity of ideas was missing from my experience. Creativity and innovation took a back seat to conformity. All the while I was meeting with middle school students who were reading at a third-grade level. It was hard to understand why I was the only one who felt an urgency about helping them read better. The clock was ticking for the Black boys I met at Freedom Readers who needed strong literacy skills as badly as they needed the next breath. Their futures depended on being able to look prospective employers in the eye and answer interview questions. Knowing how to read could set them free, could help them navigate a world where racism throws up barriers every day. I believed strongly that educational leaders had a responsibility to help them gain that skill by any means necessary.

Sometimes we miss a golden opportunity to amplify an answer because we are in love with our own reflections. As valuable as it is to turn a critical eye on the world, it is most valuable to turn that same eye on ourselves and our dedication to tradition and the way things used to be.

So after having read my dissertation and listening to my presentation, the committee raised questions about my wokeness. After about thirty minutes of this, the five of us seated at a long table in Wardlaw Hall, I was asked to step out into the hallway. I paced the corridor, nervously wringing my hands, remembering the words of my adviser the day before: "Don't be nervous. I've been doing this for decades. Your paper is stronger than many I've read, and no one has failed. Of course, no paper is perfect, and you'll probably be asked to make some adjustments. But unless there are some glaringly egregious errors in your study, I'm certain you'll hear 'Congratulations, Dr. Bailey. You've passed.'"

But when I walked back into the room, my adviser said the opposite. "The committee has discussed it and determined that you won't be moving on today. We suggest that you take a class in critical race theory and try defending again at the end of the summer. Do you have any questions?" It was early April and I had hoped to graduate in May. What I heard them say is that by the end of the summer I had to reshape myself and my paper to fit the mold they'd cast for me.

The decision came as such a shock that I couldn't think of one thing to say. I wish I had brought along a scribe, the way some people do when they know they might get bad news at the doctor's office. At least then I would have had a witness, someone to confirm that I really heard what I thought I heard. After the words were released into the air like a poison gas, I couldn't hear anything else. I could barely hold myself together long enough to gather my things and walk to the parking lot.

After driving home and thinking about my own educational journey, I wrote a very long, very direct email to the committee members, asking them to explain their position. What were the egregious errors in my paper that kept me from moving on? I addressed every one of their concerns and told them that I would not spend another semester taking classes while families were counting on me to continue providing literacy tutoring. I explained that, in my opinion, the most important work of my life involved helping prepare those children for their future. If that meant that I had to walk away with an ABD ("all but dissertation") instead of a PhD, I was fine with that.

The email reminded them of the purpose of the dissertation. It forced them to ask themselves if I had done enough in my paper to prove that I could conduct a research study. My email let them know that their decision would have to be defended in the public square, where I was prepared to appeal it. Each committee member responded that she really could not pinpoint a weakness in my research abilities. My adviser responded first, saying that my work ethic was strong, and she would be fine with seeing me move forward. Then the committee member who had recommended that I take another class in CRT admitted that I could take that class in conjunction with whatever teaching job I might obtain after graduation. A third committee member, the one who gave me thirty books from her personal collection to study on my own, responded to the group that if it was all right with everyone else, she wouldn't object to seeing me graduate in May. The entire time these messages were coming across my computer screen, my stomach was tied in knots. I knew that it only took one holdout to keep me from progressing. I waited nervously for the fourth reply all afternoon. Nothing. I went to bed that night thinking about it, but I didn't sleep a wink. I checked my messages the next morning and found that there was an email waiting for me. I took four or five deep breaths before opening it. The last professor to respond to my email wrote just a few words: "Now you sound like an advocate for the children. You can move on." And that was it. I sat in front of the screen, stunned. Walked downstairs and gave my husband the news. He smiled, hugged me, told me they had done the right thing. They reversed the decision they had handed down the day before. One day after branding me with a scarlet F, I was given the green light to move on. I graduated in May, as I had hoped.

**After receiving my degree,** I returned to Darden Terrace with renewed energy and a deeper understanding of why our program mattered. My experience with academia had taught me that the children's best interest was not always the driving force behind decisions that should ultimately benefit them, so I'm grateful that I didn't have anyone standing over me with a clipboard and pen, ready to pull my funding or shut me down if things did not proceed exactly as I'd planned. Though we struggled to find the financial support we needed to execute all our plans the way we'd like, we had a level of freedom and autonomy that comes with striking out on your own.

We learned quickly that we had to be flexible. The population was fluid at first, and many things were unpredictable to some degree, but I made a promise to myself that when the school bus pulled up outside the Daren Terrace Community Center on Monday afternoons at 2:45, I would be there to meet the kids. If it rained, I'd be there. If I was tired, I'd still show up. If half of the tutors who promised to be there with me changed their minds at the last minute, I'd still be there. And I brought my own son and daughter with me week after week because I wanted them to be exposed to people and environments that might be different from what they encountered at school. I wanted them to understand fully that they belonged to a bigger family than just the sheltered nuclear unit in their home. Seeing the way they advocate for social justice now, it's clear that at least some of the lessons made an impact.

Perhaps the early organizers of Freedom Readers were granted the liberty to try a new way of teaching and learning together because nobody really expected it to last. It's probably more likely few people even knew that we existed. Our community had a vague sense that all the students should be reading at grade level, and they knew that some were falling behind, but there was not a sustained conversation about why that was significant to our long-term health. Literacy was not at the top of the list of most people's priorities at the time, so it was up to me to raise awareness by making an unwavering commitment to the work. If I couldn't be consistent and steadfast, if I wasn't willing to walk through hell or high water to keep my word, I knew the whole thing would collapse right away. I had to look past the imperfect, the struggle, and celebrate the little victories. I had to surround myself with people who understood the importance of doing the same.

The first victory we marked was a small but noticeable increase in the positive involvement of the housing authority. At some point, I convinced the resident services coordinator to give me a key to the community center so that I could spend time there outside the weekly meetings, setting up our on-site library and hosting discussions with parents. This also kept us from having to stand outside in the cold and rain waiting for him to unlock the door each week. I understood the importance of patience, but the third time he forgot to show up to unlock the door even after I'd called to remind him, I was hot. We were losing precious reading time, and tutors were irritated and wondering if they'd made a mistake venturing into the housing projects. Kids ran through the small parking lot calling each other everything but a child of God, and a few just simply ran across the street to their apartments, never to be seen again that day. Then the resident services coordinator would roll up thirty minutes later—I can only describe his demeanor as leisurely—with a sheepish smile. "Y'all been waiting for me long?"

At that time the Darden Terrace Housing Development was a forty-year-old public housing community consisting of a hundred rent-controlled apartments and populated predominantly by African American families. Darden Terrace was just one of three developments managed by the Housing Authority of Conway (HAC). Families qualified to live there based on their income, and all heads of household had to pass a criminal background check. In addition, all residents had to be in good standing with all neighboring housing authorities. In July 2012, the HAC worked with 278 family members and ninety-seven families, and the average number of members per family was 2.87. There were twelve male heads of household and eighty-five female heads of household. There were four couples living in apartments managed by the HAC. This statistic might begin to shed some light on the absence of fathers at the All Pro Dad meeting I attended before Freedom Readers was developed.

According to housing authority officials, the unemployment rate in the community was as high as 85 percent, and the average age of the parents in the community was in the early twenties. The HAC reported that 31.96 percent of residents' primary income came from general government assistance. Other sources of income included child support, military pay, social security, and unemployment checks. In July 2012, seventy-three children between the ages of five and eleven, the ages Freedom Readers served, lived in Darden Terrace. Of the 278 residents, 259 were African American, fifteen were European American, and four were biracial.

A marble sign marked the entrance to Darden Terrace, and a playground was directly across the street and next to the community center. Children could regularly be seen sliding down slides or playing basketball. The community center where Freedom Readers was born was a single-level brick building with glass doors. There were a few parking spaces in front of the building, and there was a larger parking lot a few feet away. In some areas, trash could be seen in yards, but for the most part, streets were relatively clean. It was not uncommon to see residents congregating together in yards and on porches when the weather was nice. Many residents hung their laundry on the clotheslines that were in the backyards of all the units.

Freedom Readers was designed and implemented to support families in Darden Terrace and other nearby low-income areas as they assisted their children in achieving their academic goals in reading. Twenty students in grades kindergarten through five were enrolled on a first-come, first-served basis. Because the early volunteers conducted door-to-door canvassing events, I was able to meet many of the residents and was invited inside many of their homes. Back then there were two Freedom Readers sites, equipped to tutor as many as forty young scholars. After ten years of operation, we've expanded to twenty sites in three counties. Each of these sites offers three sessions per year: spring, summer, and fall, each lasting approximately eight to ten weeks. At each site, as many as twenty adults work one-to-one as literacy tutors to the scholars.

Literacy volunteers or tutors are trained by university literacy professors or other professionals on topics such as finding the appropriate book, keeping the scholar focused and engaged, and ways to teach reading. Our mission is to improve reading skills, not usurp the role of the classroom teacher, whose job it is to teach the child to read. We provide a space where children can practice their developing literacy skills. In this sense, we see ourselves as the classroom teacher's power booster. Most schools in our area ask parents and caregivers to read with their children for twenty minutes each evening, because we all get better at what we practice. Schools understand what a recent analysis of 174,000 PISA (Programme for International Student Assessment) scores revealed. According to a blog post from the test-provider Renaissance: "a student's level of reading engagement was more highly correlated with their reading achievement than their socioeconomic status, gender, family structure, or time spent on homework. In fact, students with the lowest socioeconomic background but high reading engagement scored better than students with the highest socioeconomic background but low reading engagement." It is also true that many families living in low-income communities may not have the luxury of reading with their children for fifteen to twenty minutes each day, for a variety of reasons. The Freedom Readers program fills in the gap for these families one afternoon each week and sends children home with books to build their home libraries. We intend to make the discovery and exploration of these high-interest books so appealing that students will be drawn to spend time reading every day.

Training is an essential component of our process. During tutors' first training meeting after joining the organization, they are told what to expect, and they are given background on the organization. A midsession training meeting gives tutors opportunities to share their unique experiences and ask for advice on how to help their specific young scholar improve in reading. Team leaders give short presentations on various topics, such as the use of graphic organizers and reader response journals, all of which can be employed by tutors during the forty-five-minute one-to-one reading time. Tutors who work with younger scholars are given some guidance in how to vary activities so that scholars stay engaged. Team leaders meet at the beginning of each session, and tutors are offered two opportunities to develop their skills. Tutors are also offered support from their team leaders, who might give informal verbal feedback or send an email with suggestions for making the time more productive.

There is one literacy volunteer assigned to work with each young scholar, and the pool of volunteers is vast and varied: parents of scholars in the program, retired educators, community members, attorneys, bankers, real estate agents, clergy, and professors and students at local universities. Tutors work with the same child at every meeting, and the partnerships remain intact for at least the duration of the session. Some partnerships have remained intact for more than four years.

Each of the twenty Freedom Readers sites is led by a team leader who is trained in how to implement themed lessons during each meeting of the session. Team leaders and tutors meet the week before the scholars begin their work to discuss the session's theme, topics such as presidents, the Olympics, or perseverance, and to become familiar with the lessons. These lessons are written in a bound lesson plan packet or theme book and are distributed to team leaders along with supporting video clips and vocabulary words. The team leaders who took over when I moved on from the Darden Terrace site to focus on expanding the program were both professionals—one is a professor of diversity studies in the education department at the local university and the other owned her own legal transcription business.

Routines have been established for each weekly meeting. When young scholars enter the building, they are given name tags and they sign in. Then they all participate in a whole group activity. This activity is followed by the viewing of various two- to three-minute video clips about the theme. Team leaders then lead discussions about the video that allow everyone in the room to reflect on key ideas. A ten-minute snack time follows, in which tutors and young scholars chat informally and prepare for one-to-one reading.

The next portion of the meeting, the heart and soul of our work, is devoted to close reading. The team leader directs the group in reading short passages each week. Tutors then ask young scholars to read to them from books that they estimate should be at the child's reading level, and then the tutor reads to the child from a book that might be above his reading level, but within his area of interest. Tutors are trained to determine which book might be best for the child, but the driving force behind book selection is always the scholar. Information gleaned from interest inventories and scholar preference is prioritized, making choice a large component of our technique. A tutor will sit with a scholar during the first meeting with a book suggested by the team leaders, but if that book seems too complex or too easy or is of little interest to the scholar, tutors help them choose another book. Team leaders suggest books for the first session that fall in one of four categories: prereading, simple texts, complex, and advanced. A small number of books are set aside in color-coded bins to assist tutors in their selection. This portion of the meeting lasts forty-five minutes, and during that time tutors and young scholars complete a variety of tasks, including preparing for speeches and choosing a new book to take home each week.

The final fifteen minutes of each meeting are set aside for young scholars to make presentations based on their reading or on questions posed by team leaders. Young scholars are provided with an outline for writing speeches as well as criteria for evaluating their own performance. No scholar is forced to participate in this activity, but they are strongly encouraged to do so. When the session begins, only a few young people will raise their hands to give speeches, but by the middle of the session just about every scholar volunteers. On the last week of the session, team leaders generally need to come up with a system to choose who is called forward first, because most of the scholars want it to be them. When the speeches are over the meeting ends, and the young scholars head home with books they select from the take-home table on their way out.

I carefully mapped out every moment of the program to reflect the research I encountered during my doctoral studies. Not one opportunity to engage young minds is wasted. The ninety minutes we spend together is fast-paced, and the activities are varied and tailored to the skill level of each child. Above all else, the program creates opportunities for young people to lead, find their voices, and outgrow themselves. That can only be possible when the stakeholders fully embrace the vision, align themselves with our values and beliefs, and invest their resources in realizing the dream. Our key partners set the tone for our work and are largely responsible for any success we've enjoyed. Some of them have been involved since the beginning, and others have come and gone. We've found, however, that somehow the right people show up for the right job every time.

# CHAPTER FOUR

I t wasn't exactly love at first sight. I was a skinny, knobby-kneed seventeen-year-old with glasses and a pigtail, wandering around the campus of the College of Charleston alone, when he extended his hand and introduced himself. He wore a white Miami Hurricanes hat and a wide grin that I would encounter many times that summer. We were two of 250 students from around South Carolina participating in the Governor's School for Academics, a five-week residential program for kids with good grades and bright futures. After shaking his hand and learning his name, Ike, I walked the bricked-lined streets with my head down, thinking about the boyfriend I'd left behind in my hometown. This would be my first time away from him since we started dating three months earlier. When I left home that Saturday morning, I had said goodbye to my parents and was getting ready to find my way in a strange environment, something I'd never done before. On the one-hour ride from home to Charleston, I rested my head against the window and cried silently the entire time.

It took me a while to get used to the whole thing: the college dorms we slept in, the shared bathrooms, the professors and the college-level classes they taught, the dining hall. Coming from a dirt-roads community on the outskirts of a town few could find on a map, it felt more like I had been dropped onto the surface of the moon than an experience that was supposed to be enriching and fun. But as the days progressed, I occasionally fell in with a group of Black kids who made me feel more comfortable than being alone. Ike was a part of that group. We'd get together in the evenings before curfew to play cards or watch TV in someone's room. Sometimes I'd join that crowd, and other times I'd venture off by myself. It wasn't that I didn't like those kids. Complete comfort eluded me, because I couldn't shake the thought that I didn't really belong there. I didn't feel smart enough, and thought my clothes were a little too "last season."

Above all else I didn't feel pretty enough, thanks to the group of girls who had ridden my school bus years earlier and made it their mission to proclaim loudly to the world that they thought I was ugly. Adolescence had brought with it a severe case of acne that those girls found endlessly entertaining. They were older and louder and traveled together in a pack, maybe five of them in all. I was an awkward kid in middle school when those high school girls focused their teasing on me, and there were no older brothers, sisters, or cousins to come to my defense or even guarantee victory if I stood up for myself. Once they saw that I wouldn't respond to their taunting, which brought thunderous laughter from their captive audience, they tortured me the entire time we were on the bus together. Ten minutes might sound like a short time, but it can feel like forever when the only sound on a crowded school bus with seats packed three deep is laughter at your expense.

The thought of talking to an adult about the bullying made my stomach churn with embarrassment. Like any typical teenage girl, I wanted to fit in more than anything. I didn't want to have acne, so I spent as little time as possible acknowledging it. Whenever someone brought it up, I did my best to change the subject. But the teasing was really taking a toll on me. One day I gathered up the nerve to ask my mother what to do.

"Them girls are just jealous of you," she said. "You need to just ignore them. They'll go away."

Only they didn't. And as the days passed, they grew bolder in their taunting, as if they thought about me during the school day when they should have been taking notes in geography class. I began making up excuses to stay after school so I wouldn't have to face them. When I couldn't find another way home, I'd pick a seat next to a window and bury my head in a book, but I can't remember reading one page. Though I acted like I couldn't hear their taunts and the laughter it evoked, every word penetrated my armor. In the middle of what was the most challenging season of my life to that point, a season where it seemed that there was no one in my life who cared enough or had enough strength to shield me from daily humiliation, I turned to the most powerful coping mechanism I knew. It was taught to me from the time I was in the cradle and drilled into my head on a weekly basis. I turned to prayer and asked God to take away my acne so that I could be beautiful.

It never crossed my mind to fight those girls back, with words or fists. There's no question in my mind that had I resisted, things would have escalated and become physical in a hurry. The bus driver was a high schooler himself, and as a rule ignored the goings-on of the students unless there was a fight he had to report. In one sense, I simply felt outnumbered, intimidated, and afraid. The minute I stepped on that bus, my voice disappeared the same way I tried to make myself disappear. On another level, and in a small corner of my heart, I believed those girls were right. I was too ugly for anyone to look at, the pimples on my face did make me intolerable. Their voices began to shape my self-image. The story they told me about who I was and what I was worth started to translate into what I told myself about myself. For young girls like me, this is the valley of the shadow of death.

Eventually, the girls graduated. The ringleader was a senior the year I was targeted. The singling out on the bus stopped when she left, but that on-guard feeling, that burning shame about my appearance, did not. When I heard about the Governor's School from a senior at my high school who had attended the summer before, it felt like liberation, a chance to start again, where no one knew my name and I could be seen for what I could do academically, not how I looked. She visited all the Advanced Placement classes to talk about her experience and drum up interest. I knew immediately that I wanted to go. I picked up the forms from the guidance office and showed them to my dad. He said he thought it would be a good opportunity for me, but he couldn't afford the application fee. Fortunately, there was financial assistance for prospects like me. My family paid a small amount of the tuition, and the Governor's School covered the rest. As I participated in activities and continued to meet new people, I realized that some of them were in the same situation as me, but it wasn't our clothes that signaled our scholarship status. Every now and then I'd be in a conversation with someone who'd spent the past summer in Paris, or who had taken a ski trip with their family the winter before. Those were the kids with parents who were politicians, doctors, lawyers, and college professors. Surely none of them needed financial aid to secure their spot, and the thought made me feel second-class. I loved that we were all there together, though. At least we were being given a chance to learn about and from one another. Though I may have felt out of place at times, I knew no one could send me home.

By the time the summer ended, I had developed a complicated and intense relationship with Ike, the boy with the wide grin and the Miami Hurricanes hat who had extended his hand to me on the first day. The first hurdle involved Marsha, a girl with beautiful hazel eyes and an unforgettable southern twang who befriended me during the first week of the program. She said yes when I asked if she wanted to walk to dinner together. We talked about the crazy expectations of the professors and the cute boys in the group. I told her about the crush I had on a light-skinned boy from the Upstate who seemed to look right through me when he walked by, and she revealed to me that she only had eyes for one boy.

"These boys around here are fine and they know they fine. All of them seem stuck up to me, except this one boy. I want to talk to him, but I'm not sure he's trying to hear me," she confided in me as we shared a table near the back of the dining hall.

"Well, if he doesn't want to talk to you, that would be his loss. Why don't you just walk up to him and ask him?"

"I can't do that! What if he disses me in front of everybody? What am I supposed to do then?"

"Diss him back! Wait a minute. Who are we talking about anyway? Is it somebody I know?"

"Yep. He sure is. I know you know him because I saw him walk into your autobiography class the other day. Hey, I have an idea. Since he's in your class, just talk to him for me. Find out if he's feeling me at all."

"In my class? Who are you talking about? There are a lot of boys in my class, girlfriend."

"But the only one I want to talk to is sitting right over there."

I turned my head and saw Ike sitting over a tray overflowing with food and three glasses of red juice. He was too wrapped up his conversation to notice us looking, but Marsha fussed at me anyway.

"Turn around before he figures out that we're talking about him, girl! You trying to put all my business on front street?"

"No, no, sorry. Plus, that boy is not paying any attention to us at all. Yeah, now that I look at him a little closer, I guess he might be cute. He's really nice, though. Approachable, I can say that about him. I'll talk to him for you, but that class doesn't meet for another three days. Why don't we just look him up in the directory and call him tonight? We're not going to be in this program forever, you know. We have to move fast if you plan to make a love connection before it's time to go home."

"OK. That might work. At eight o'clock tonight, you call him and find out if he likes me. You call me right after that and let me know, all right?"

"Sure. Girl, I don't know why you too scary to call him yourself. Whatever, though. I'm happy to pull back my arrow and be the Cupid you need to get this party started."

I called him that night. His roommate answered the phone and passed it along to Ike. I told him who I was, made a little light chitchat about the American Autobiography class, and noticed he was a bit quiet, his answers very brief. I finally got around to explaining the reason for my call with a kind of boldness I never would have had at home. This was about Marsha. I had absolutely nothing to lose.

"Listen, my friend Marsha told me to give you a call and see if you like her. She likes you and she told me to call and let you know, so what you gone do about it?"

His answer shocked me. Ike told me on the phone that night that he wasn't going to do anything about Marsha.

"The girl I like is you," he said. I held the phone to my ear for a few more seconds and then babbled a few sounds, like "Uh, OK." I hung up the phone fast and sat on my bed staring at the wall. The call had not gone as I had imagined. Not only had Ike's response been the opposite of what I had expected, the way he delivered the news was an even bigger surprise. His words did not flow together fluently through the phone line. It had taken him several minutes to get the words out, interrupted by stops and starts and sounds that didn't belong. *The girl I like is you.* I understood what he was telling me, but I had never heard anyone speak the way he did. We didn't talk about it much that summer, but he later explained that he'd developed a severe stutter when he was eight. He'd had all kinds of speech therapy, but everything he tried only made it worse. His stutter had never been an issue in our exchanges before. He'd figured out how to respond to questions quickly, before the stutter could catch up with him. And that smile that came off as so charming on the day we met was a part of a coping mechanism that made it easier for people to answer their own questions, while he kept smiling and gave the stutter less of a chance to steal the show. The smile was much less effective on the phone, and the stutter stepped forward and loomed large in that domain. What would take another boy two minutes to say took him so long that I squirmed in my chair, developed sweat stains under my arms, and gave my roommate a funny look. I was confused by the way he talked at first, didn't really know how to categorize it. All I knew for sure was that the way he talked made him different. It meant that he would stand out, and if the kids at Governor's School were anything like the kids I had known at home, he would be singled out. Things could potentially get brutal. I was at the Governor's School to get away from ridicule. But his words echoed nonetheless: *The girl I like is you.* Marsha called me later that night to find out what had happened.

"Oh, I called, and his roommate said he wasn't there."

Somewhere along the line I learned that like me, Ike was one of the scholarship babies. That made me feel more comfortable in his presence, although his stutter still made me squirm. Then one night about halfway through the program after a boisterous spades game in someone's dorm room, he offered to walk me back to the third floor. We took the stairs, and before I could open the door to the hallway, he grabbed me and kissed me. It threw me off, because I was trying to keep my distance, both out of respect and loyalty to the boyfriend I left at home and the desire to avoid teasing by association. I shouldn't have worried much about the ridicule, though. It turned out the Guvvies didn't care much about the way Ike talked. They embraced him with open arms in a way that astonished me. Whenever he walked into an assembly the entire room yelled out, "IIIIkkkkkeeeee!!" It reminded me of the show *Cheers*, and the way everybody greeted and loved Norm. To my amazement, he turned out to be one of the most popular kids in the group.

When Governor's School graduation day arrived, the tears I cried were a sign that I had gone from a not-so-sure-about-this kid to a fully invested girl in just five weeks. Ike was always there, always smiling and welcoming, and I was always happy to see that smile. We became friends because that one magical, summer of freedom made it possible for me to slow down and listen to what he had to say, stutter and all. He made me laugh, he was spontaneous, and he surprised me all the time with some goofy dance move or by picking me up off the floor and holding me over his head like King Kong while I screamed bloody murder and all our friends laughed. I made it clear that I wasn't interested in going further, but that changed on the very last day of the program, when we were allowed to stay up all night. We walked by the ocean and he showed me the constellations he learned about in astronomy class. He pointed at the stars with one hand and reached for mine with the other. I didn't pull away. For the most part, he kept the flirting to a minimum, but he didn't stop seeking me out. I loved talking with him about the wonder of our summer experience and about the things that fascinated me and made me wonder and worried me. Nobody listened like Ike.

It's hard to put into words what those five weeks meant to me in terms of exposure. There were guest speakers, concert pianists, and movies about environmental conservation that we viewed and discussed. The night before graduation, girls wore their prom dresses to the governor's ball and boys put on ties and fancy shoes for the first time all summer. We danced the night away in the Stern Center ballroom. I went with Ike and two other kids from our American Autobiography class. (Ike had asked me to go as his date, but I told him that we should all go as a group. That would be more fun and much easier to explain to my boyfriend back home.) And during one important assembly, the state's governor at the time, Carroll Campbell, came to address us. I was thoroughly impressed by the questions some of our fellow Guvvies asked and the confidence with which they spoke. We were seventeen years old. You would have thought members of the White House press corps occupied those seats.

In my American Autobiography class, I met more of the intellectually intriguing voices that would mentor me. I read Maya Angelou and Maxine Hong Kingston, and Alex Haley's *Autobiography of Malcolm X*. I watched films about Harvey Milk and Janice Joplin that are so vivid in my mind thirty years later I can quote lines from them by heart. Those five weeks changed the way I thought, the way I read, the way I engaged with the world. Looking back, I'm reminded of the way Frederick Douglass described standing on the balcony of the Baltimore plantation house where he lived, watching the billowing white sails of ships in the distance. They spoke of possibility, of a life far different from the one he'd known. They renewed his hope and stoked a fire and a longing to be free. The ten books on the syllabus of that one class were my sailboats.

We all returned home at the end of the summer, and Ike kept his promise to stay in touch. He wrote me letters and invited me to come see him perform in pageants and play football and hang out with his friends. He only lived an hour away, so I guess it was possible to accept his invitations if my parents approved, but I had gone back to dating the boyfriend I hadn't wanted to leave in the first place. I didn't put a stop to things completely, because an insecure teenager like me feasted on the attention. For years I sent mixed messages. He went off to Davidson College on a football scholarship while I went back to Charleston to earn a degree in English. He would drive more than three hours to Charleston to take me to the movies after I reluctantly agreed to see him. Everything in me wanted to run the other way. I didn't want my friends to meet him and associate me with someone who was less than perfect. That was the ideal I tried to attain. If I could have perfect grades and perfect hair and be perfectly funny in every situation, I wouldn't be rejected. That was my reasoning in those days. Nothing changed until seven years into our relationship, when Ike called me one day out of the blue to deliver news that I didn't expect. We'd graduated college and were trying to find our way in the world as adults. He was an intern at the public relations office at Davidson College, and I was teaching English at the local high school.

"I need to talk to you." His tone was serious. Most of our conversations had been me doing most of the talking, so his taking the lead was new.

"OK. Should I sit down?"

"Doesn't really matter. Just want you to know that I've been doing a lot of thinking. You say you want to be friends, but I'm ready for something more. You don't seem to want that with me. I've met someone else. She has a daughter, and I really like her, so there's no need for you to call me anymore. This is goodbye."

"Goodbye? What do you mean?"

"Means what I said. Don't call me anymore. It's just going to be better for the both of us if we move on."

It was this turn of events that facilitated my miraculous change of heart. Let's just call it a come to Jesus moment. He'd implied that he was tired of me and my hot-and-cold behavior a few times before, but he always called the next day. This time, I didn't hear from him at all. When I tried to call, he'd listen to my recap of the day, sit silently on the line for a few minutes and make up an excuse to get off the phone. It didn't take long for me to physically feel the ache of his absence from my life. He had been there for me for years, listening to all my secrets and worries, while I had placed appearances above his feelings. I never laughed when my friends or family members said something negative about the way he talked, but I didn't rush to his defense either. I was a weak, self-centered coward who had lost a beautiful gem. It would take some doing, but I had to get him back.

I made a list of creative ways to say I was sorry, and showed him more respect in a few months than I had in all the years we'd known each other. In time, he softened, and the relationship he'd developed with a coworker became less of a priority. By that time he was a tall, muscular, and handsome former college-football player with a gym addiction. And when most young men his age were playing the field, he was up-front about his desire to settle down and get married. When we admitted that we were both broken and hurting in different ways, but that maybe the only way we could heal was together, I allowed myself to relax and trust him, and accept him with his imperfections, as I tried to accept my own. What the stutter stole from him in smooth talk he more than made up for in chivalry and gallantry. After all we'd been through, I knew beyond all doubt that inside his chest beat a strong, courageous heart. He was all transparency and vulnerability, and called forth the goodness in my nature. When I weighed the pros and cons, the choice was undeniably clear. We were married almost exactly eight years to the day after he extended his hand to me wearing that Hurricanes cap. No, it wasn't love at first sight, but it has turned into the love of a lifetime.

**Once we reached stable footing** and worked through a lot of our drama, our conversations and dreams circled back to the place where we met, the Governor's School for Academics at the College of Charleston. We revisited the transformative moments, the people we met and the books we read there that changed us. We said to each other that if we ever found ourselves in a financial position where we could give back, we'd create a similar experience for kids from dirt-roads communities like the ones that had given birth to us.

When the conditions were right for Freedom Readers to be born, we were ready. We questioned our readiness on days when our bank account was strained to the point of breaking, as we tried to make ends meet on one income after having become accustomed to two, but when it came to the core of our philosophical standing, our hearts beat in sync. There was the issue of some of our younger family members who were making choices that brought them into contact with the criminal justice system. We watched this and it pained us. We felt young and invincible and thought that with our high-dollar educations we had the power to make things right, somehow. We knew that we couldn't just keep getting fat on the rights our mothers and fathers had gained. We needed our own activism, the kind that helped individuals achieve their dreams while putting pressure on systems to become more equitable and just. We couldn't pay back the '60s Freedom Fighters, but we could try to reach back for another generation. Freedom Readers would end up being a part of our strategy of doing our part and giving back to our community. We agreed that we would use whatever tools we found at our disposal to make a difference. We would create an experience for young people that was first class, that piqued their curiosity and helped them answer the questions that simmered just beneath the surface of their minds. We would remind them of their inherent beauty and brilliance and potential. We'd attempt to make use of our brokenness and turn it into a way to heal.

For the first three years of our marriage, we focused on enjoying each other and building our professional lives. We were both so ambitious and hungry to prove to ourselves and the world that we deserved a seat at the table. We didn't hesitate to put in long hours and push the envelope when it came to the status quo. Ike would blaze a trail in journalism, writing a well-read, award-winning column in the local paper for more than a decade. By the time he was hired by the *Sun News*, I had already started a teaching career at Socastee High School. When our son came along after I had been teaching high school English for five years, we decided that one of us would always be at home with our kids. We knew we wouldn't be able to give them millions of dollars in a trust fund when they were grown, but we could give them a nurturing home and good guidance while they were small. My last day as a full-time high school teacher was the day before our son was born.

## CHAPTER FIVE

Gospel music filled room 323 of the Fine Arts Center at the College of Charleston every Wednesday night from 6:30 to 8:30. Our director, Jonifer Q. Fashion, sat behind the piano in the rehearsal room and began with warm-ups. *Ma May Me Mo Moo.* I'd never had any vocal training before that, had never really thought much about how voices came together to form harmonies. When I was growing up in the Mt. Zion AME Church, we were a conscripted choir, enlisted by our mothers to get up and sing on the designated Sunday. Our director was spirited and quite talented, but the only singing rules I'd known in my church were "Sing loud, and don't chew gum." The adults didn't care so much about the quality of the sound we produced; it was the spirit that mattered most. That's one of the things I appreciate most about my Gullah roots. As descendants of enslaved Africans who toiled on rice, indigo, and cotton plantations, we Gullahs expressed our deep emotions through music. It has been a kind of therapy for our people, and as such has prioritized honesty and authenticity above all else. This is how gospel music was given to me as a child. All of that would change as my time as a College of Charleston Gospel Choir member progressed and we learned to blend our voices in a way that would make audiences weep.

The choir members came from Black churches all over the state, with diverse styles of worship and beliefs, some Baptist, some Pentecostal, some Holiness, some AME. My suitemate was the first person I'd met from an Apostolic church. You could tell who came from a home church that emphasized contemporary music like the songs we were learning. Those choir members, especially the seniors, would make sure that we were hitting every note correctly and that our sound was as close to the recording as possible. They were concerned with the professionalism of the group, while I was just happy to have a safe space on campus where I could relax and feel at home. We could be ourselves and wrap ourselves in messages that had once buoyed our ancestors when they needed encouragement. In keeping with the gospel music trends of the time, our choir put a modern spin on the songs that had given the Black community life, hope, and joy for centuries.

I looked forward to our performances with nervousness and great anticipation. I hoped that I could remember all the words—there were eight or nine new songs to learn for concerts. It helped that I was one of about eighty-five voices, all of us dressed in black, most of us dealing with the same level of anxious anticipation. I sang with the altos, who often occupied the right side of the risers brought into the concert hall for the occasion.

Singing with my college choir is what I missed most two years after I graduated from C of C, when Ike and I joined the evangelical church where Freedom Readers would take its first breath. About 90 percent of the congregants were white when we joined in 1998, which made me a bit uneasy when I visited the first time, because it was so different from what I'd known church to be all my life. We pushed past those reservations in the beginning partly because the Sunday service didn't last three to four hours like Ike's home church, causing him to miss a good chunk of the football games he wanted to watch on TV. We were in and out in less than ninety minutes, and that worked for me. Beyond that, though, we often commented on the ride home that parts of the sermons reached us on a deep level. The lessons that were taught from the pulpit were easy to follow and challenged the areas of our hearts that were selfish, greedy, and lacked compassion for others. But there was also a very affirming tone to the messages which introduced us to a loving God who accepted us despite our flaws. To a couple of self-proclaimed misfits, these words were music to our ears and assured us that we had finally found a place where we could belong. I took copious notes during those sermons and studied them during the week. I looked up the scriptures that were referenced and emailed church leaders to find out more about concepts I didn't understand. It was during this period that I developed a daily spiritual practice that included prayer and reflection. My husband and I were both making positive changes.

Although a large portion of what we gained in the early days of our membership was beneficial, not every aspect of our experience was good. The vibe was different from what we'd known growing up, which constantly forced us to choose a style of worship that made others comfortable. We loved our church enough to try to be a part of making it better for everyone, especially those who came from backgrounds like ours, so we summoned the courage to speak up. The resulting friction could be ignored for a time, but would never be fully resolved.

We'd grown up with sermons that positioned Scripture as a tool of the resistance and emphasized Christianity's liberating power. Gospel music and the message of those sermons were critical weapons in the fight to overcome the hardships of racism, poverty, and overall struggle. We'd grown up with music that lifted our spirits and spoke the language of our heartbeats because it was born of the mournful cries of the enslaved and was coded with messages of freedom. As I interpreted the situation, this new church we had joined often focused instead on the writings of the Apostle Paul, who emphasized being content with your current station in life. This "bloom where you're planted" theology included a healthy dose of spiritual authority teaching, backed by New Testament scriptures reminding us that our job as Christians was to submit to the governance of whoever was placed in power over us. Those people were placed in positions of authority by God to teach us and help us grow spiritually. Even if they did not realize it, abusive leaders were being used by God and could be His divine mouthpiece. One of the cornerstones of this philosophy came from Paul's teachings in Romans 8:28: *And we know that all things work together for good to them that love God, to them who are the called according to his purpose.* By this logic, there was really no need to get too upset about anything a leader did or said, because in the end it would be used by God to promote you. No matter how awful the leader, we were taught to serve with humility and grace until such time that God chose to elevate us as a reward for our steadfast obedience.

Years later, this teaching made it easy, almost necessary, for white evangelicals to embrace Donald Trump and his racist rhetoric. It puzzled me at first how a man who bragged about sexually assaulting women could be even remotely palatable for people who proclaimed to follow Jesus, but it all makes perfect sense now. Churchgoers had been primed since birth to receive Trump with open arms, to overlook his character flaws and see in him a savior. Some white evangelicals didn't need much convincing, because his racism appealed to them outright. Others wrestled with the idea of allowing such a morally bankrupt person to represent them and ended up going back to what they had always been taught. *All things work together for the good . . .*

Somehow, though, that spiritual authority argument didn't hold up quite as well when Obama was in office. There were whispers among members of my church that he was the actual Antichrist.

For ninety minutes on Sunday morning, I gave up the gospel music that still fed my soul at home and in my car for a brand of Christian rock that bore no resemblance to the melodies that empowered me. The white majority was different from us in a million ways, yet we had one thing in common. Most of us southern-born members in that church could trace our ancestry back to the kinds of plantations that had existed on the very land the church occupied. But while their fathers held the whip on that plantation, our fathers bore the lash.

Opinion polls conducted by the Public Religion Research Institute reflect the legacy of this shared history and its impact on Christianity today. For instance, its 2018 American Values Survey showed that church-affiliated whites are more likely to deny the existence of structural racism than their non-church-affiliated counterparts. Furthermore, whites who attend church more often tend to reject the idea of structural racism even more vehemently than those who only attend occasionally. Churchgoing whites are twice as likely to say that the killings of Black men by police are isolated incidents rather than evidence of a pattern of discrimination against African Americans. These attitudes can be traced back to the rituals of white supremacy that have played themselves out in houses of worship since the founding of this nation. In contrast to the warm welcome we and other African Americans receive in some white evangelical churches today, it was a common practice for plantation owners and their families to bring enslaved Africans with them to church and make them sit in the back pews or in balconies reserved just for them. Such racist practices provide the foundations for how some white Christians understand and embody their faith.

Leaving the Black church was a risky, gutsy move that would be interpreted by some of our friends and relatives as a move toward elitism. Had we gone to college and come back with a sense that we were too good for own community? Would we be shunned for stepping away from what we'd always known? We didn't make the decision lightly. Ike and I prayed about it and discussed it at length before raising our hands one Sunday morning to become members. We were drawn to this church because of our personal commitment to social justice and their stated objective of bringing about racial reconciliation. We were convinced that to bring about the beloved community Dr. King imagined, we would need to try something different from what our parents and grandparents did. Sacrifices would have to be made on both sides, we reasoned. We would start by putting aside everything we knew about church from our past to embrace a new style of worship. It would be worth it to bring into existence what Reconstruction in the South could not. Racial equality. If it was going to be possible anywhere, it would be in the church, where miracles were expected. We chose to be the guinea pigs of church desegregation without studying the stories of our elders, who had suffered greatly desegregating schools, and without fully grasping the white church's deep roots in white supremacy.

We didn't know at the time that that sacrifice would always be a one-way street, and that we were expected to pave the roads. There would be no letting go of comfort on the part of the whites in the church at all, unless you count the discomfort some of the members felt at seeing us there. Our presence was treated like an appendix to the real mission of the church. Our concerns were treated like secondary issues that didn't need to be addressed head-on but that would eventually work themselves out. Once a year, during Black History Month, a Black minister would be invited to give a sermon. And although the worship team, which consisted of a few singers and a raucous band, always had a Black member, one of them would tell us later that her input concerning song choice was often ignored.

The situation quickly became tense for us, but we remained committed, because we looked to the example of the abolitionists, who endured great hardship but who finally did achieve liberation. We held a picture of John Lewis, beaten in the head by police on the Edmund Pettus Bridge, in the front of our minds. We heard the words Frederick Douglass wrote in 1857 echo in our spirits: "If there is no struggle, there is no progress." So we continued to push.

Some of the people we worshiped with and loved like family and who embraced us on so many levels continued to hold antiquated views on race that sadden me even more today than when I first encountered them. When I consider the strong negative response we got whenever we pushed too hard on the issue of race, I'm reminded of the stories Frederick Douglass recounted about the plantation owners who claimed to be fully devoted followers of Christ. What could they seriously know about a Christ who died for the sins of all when they believed that they had the right to own another person? These men held the whip in one hand and the Bible in the other, and not one aspect of this dichotomy gave them pause. Douglass railed passionately against many things in his speeches and writings, but nothing irked him more than the so-called Christian slaveholder:

> What I have said respecting and against religion, I mean strictly to apply to the *slaveholding religion* of this land, and with no possible reference to Christianity proper; for, between the Christianity of this land, and the Christianity of Christ, I recognize the widest possible difference—so wide, that to receive the one as good, pure, and holy, is of necessity to reject the other as bad, corrupt, and wicked. To be the friend of the one, is of necessity to be the enemy of the other. I love the pure, peaceable, and impartial Christianity of Christ: I therefore hate the corrupt, slaveholding, women-whipping, cradle-plundering, partial and hypocritical Christianity of this land. Indeed, I can see no reason, but the most deceitful one, for calling the religion of this land Christianity. I look upon it as the climax of all misnomers, the boldest of all frauds, and the grossest of all libels.

It can be argued that this slaveholding religion lives at the very root of today's white evangelical church. The poison swallowed by pre–Civil War congregations still flows through the branches of the tree. Our church made a point of writing into its original charter a desire to right the wrongs of racism, to appear to reject that corruption. The founders of our church may not have realized the strong influence of the past on our present-day interactions and choices. I can clearly see now that the same thinking that allowed white men to weep as they spoke from the pulpit of the unconditional love of Christ frees some of today's evangelicals to support and make excuses for a racist leader like Trump. James Baldwin said it best in the words quoted in the 2017 film *I Am Not Your Negro*: "History is not the past. It is the present. We carry our history with us. We are our history. If we pretend otherwise, we are literally criminals."

As time went on, I noticed a blurring of the lines between politics and Christianity. The label *Christian* began to take on elements that were the opposite of my identity. We didn't fit the mold, but I hoped that in a church where I initially thought everyone could find a place to belong, the teachings of love, brotherhood, and inclusion would win out over everything else. Although I saw how different our foundational beliefs were on so many fronts, I tried to keep an open mind and consider that there still might be some middle ground. We had study groups and book discussions and tried to respectfully talk things through. The church leadership supported the idea of staying engaged and said that we didn't have to see eye to eye on every issue in order to worship together.

This agree to disagree view of moving forward may have some merit, but there are also issues that are complete deal-breakers. Racism is one of them. Many members of my church believed strongly in the myth of American meritocracy. Those who do not take advantage of the boundless opportunity to succeed that America presents have only themselves to blame. In their view, there may be some racist people in this country, but systems themselves have changed so much since the 1950s that talking about institutionalized racism is just needlessly dredging up the past. Funny how the same people who wave the Confederate flag saying that they want to honor their ancestors turn around and tell Black people to forget that their ancestors were ever enslaved and that enslavement has led to an uneven playing field today.

Ike pulled way back, visited other churches, and even stayed home on Sunday mornings, but I continued to hope that on some level we would see some progress. I'd pack up my kids and take them to church every Sunday morning without fail. Every now and then we'd see a glimmer of hope, like the gospel choir from the local university coming out to sing during a worship service. Then the excitement would wane, and the leaders would lose interest, like the air going out of a balloon. Attention would turn to the next building project or sermon series, leaving us disappointed and dejected all over again. In this way, my experience with that church mirrors our national conversation on race since the founding of this country. For every Emancipation Day there has been a reign of terror, a Ku Klux Klan. For every civil rights movement, a wave of discriminatory policies and police brutality. One step forward, four steps back, with frustration mounting at every turn.

It might sound odd, but after all that we'd experienced there, I still did not hesitate to bring Freedom Readers to the world through the womb of that imperfect church twelve years after we first walked through the doors. The leaders fully embraced the idea, and in so doing gave everyone else permission to take part. I thought there were important lessons that could be learned by leaving the bubble of the sanctuary and walking out our faith together, in the places where we were most needed. At the same time, I recognized that the contradictions and ideological tensions in the church were problematic. Beneath the thin veneer of unity and tranquility, an internal war raged between the church's continual assertion that it wanted racial reconciliation and the simultaneous belief held by some conservative members that racism wasn't real. I thought that I could offer a way that leaned closer to the side of equity and social justice, and that maybe those lessons wouldn't fall on deaf ears. Freedom Readers gave me a chance to make the stated values of the church come to life the best way I knew how. To my mind, it could be a giant step forward for the church while reconnecting me to my roots. But there was so much I needed to learn as well. Some lessons came at a higher price than others.

Race, power, and privilege weren't the only topics we discussed at Freedom Readers, but we touched on them often, because the first locations we served were in the middle of local public housing communities, and almost all of the scholars who participated were Black. A large percentage of our early tutors were white. Volunteers participated in meetings hosted by Freedom Readers where we tried to unpack the implications of our racial dynamics, but I believe that the most important work took place internally as potential tutors reflected on our conversations and their motives for getting involved. There must have been complex interior calculations that led this mostly white group to accept this invitation. Very few of the fifteen original volunteers at Team Darden were strangers to me. My friend Cindy, who had invited me to be the guest speaker at the All Pro Dad breakfast about six months before, was the team captain there. That meant that she helped me stay organized and keep the kids focused and engaged. She would also step in to lead a session if I had to be away.

After several weeks of planning and extensive training, the day finally arrived for us to hold our first meeting with Team Darden. I asked the tutors to arrive early, so that we would be prepared when the bus dropped the scholars off at the door. I made place cards and placed them on the tables around the room so that everyone would know where to sit. There would be no segregation, with factions on opposite sides of the room. One adult would sit next to one child and start a conversation. The children formed a line at the door, and Cindy and I would send them to sit in the empty chair next to their scholar.

In those first days, it was almost impossible to get the balance of tutors and scholars right. Some days we'd have a big crowd of registered children show up, and I'd have to ask some tutors to work with two or three children. On other days we had adults sitting alone because there were no children. Stabilizing numbers in a one-to-one program is always a major concern.

Another challenge was managing the expectations of all the tutors in the room. Many came with their own agenda and their own ideas about how things should work. Some wanted us to teach Bible stories, so that the children might be saved by the healing power of Christ. The idea that children in the program be given religious instruction was one that I heard repeatedly. After all, one of the major tenets of our faith involved spreading the gospel to all the world. It makes sense that members of my church who felt strongly about sharing their faith would make this request. I resisted it because I wanted the program to be a place of opportunity focused on literacy. It never felt like my place to impose my religion on young children and their families. Once they gained the ability to read well, they could take that freedom and pursue whatever was best for them. The focus of the work and the emphasis on Christian principles needed to be enacted through true charity, not preached. At that point, it seemed to me that there had already been too much talking and not enough taking care of what was most crucial, the children's ability to fall in love with reading and perform well on reading tests and report cards. It was an increase in their academic achievement that would allow them to qualify for the kinds of classes that would make it easier for them to go to college or choose to enter the profession of their choice straight out of high school. Better reading skills would lead to more freedom.

Beyond my insistence that Christianity be walked out through Freedom Readers instead of talked out was my discomfort with the way slaveholders had used the Bible to keep the enslaved in a place of obedience. Using the Scriptures to justify the most heinous institution known to man is a sin for which the church has yet to atone. As Douglass wrote, there are two kinds of Christianity at question here, one that is pure and uplifting and freeing, and another that makes one man master over another. Although the possibility existed, I never wanted to knowingly sit a scholar with a tutor who openly subscribed to the latter.

When Freedom Readers was in its fourth year, it became impossible for me to reconcile my own Blackness with the dysfunctional relationship our church had with race. I found myself circling around the central question of my life in those days. Do I try to change things from the inside of this institution I love despite its issues? Or do I walk away to protect my mental health? Am I hearing a true call from God to make a difference here, or is it just my need for their conditional validation and acceptance taking charge? How much of my sanity, peace of mind, and simple self-respect do I sacrifice for this cause? How much is too much?

Ike and I fully realized that a culture is invisible to those who live within it. What hope was there of change when only a few Black members thought anything needed to change? Some Black members said they thought everything was fine in the church and that race didn't matter to them. "Focus on God," the leadership told us. "If you will simply lay your rights aside and focus on Christ, trust his plan for your life, you will find so much peace. God is in control of this situation. He'll work it out when it's time."

As hard as it was to make the decision to join the church, it was much harder to leave after sixteen years. Walking that tightrope was exhausting, and when I walked out the door for the last time, I felt a complicated mixture of overwhelming loss and grief and a burden-lifting relief. I sat in my car and turned up one of my favorite gospel songs. I imagined being back on that stage with my choir and sang at the top of my lungs. "No weapon formed against me / Shall prosper, it won't work."

# CHAPTER SIX

When it comes to reforming our education system so that it adequately meets the needs of children who have historically underachieved, nothing is more significant than the power of the collective. That power can take a small effort and magnify it to such a degree that it begins to take on a life and an energy of its own. Picture in your mind a spider. As I write this, spring is unfolding outside my window, with its longer days and brilliant sunrises. In the part of the country where I live, we see spiders quite often this time of year, spinning their webs, catching their prey, laying their eggs. Imagine walking along outside and inadvertently walking into the thread of a spiderweb. You can't see it, but there is no doubt that you have encountered it. Normally, we just wipe it away and don't give it much more thought, but let's dwell here a moment. Imagine the same scenario, but add a hundred spiderwebs, a thousand, a million. Our reaction would be quite different. In fact, I would argue that even the strongest person reading this would be stopped in her tracks. What I have just described is the core of an old Ethiopian proverb: "When spiderwebs unite, they can tie up a lion." Think about it. One of the fiercest animals alive, commonly known as the King of the Jungle, can be completely immobilized by something as fragile and as seemingly innocuous as a spiderweb. But not just any spiderweb. Spiderwebs united.

This is the principle that we often fail to activate when it comes to educating the youth of our nation. Somehow, we keep missing opportunities to form collectives, to collaborate in ways that can support children who are facing challenging situations. We recognize that solutions exist, but we miss the mark when we fall under the spell of the idea that we can do it alone. Problems as long-standing and pervasive as the ones we see in America's schools need to be addressed with the most innovative ideas, inexhaustible energy, and boundless hope. It is when we stay trapped in the same cycles with the same programs expecting different results that we find ourselves repeating history.

Fortunately, when we survey this country's educational landscape, we find many examples of collectives and collaborations that have worked. Take, for instance, the I Promise

School, which was started in 2018 by the LeBron James Family Foundation. In this instance you have a celebrity, arguably the best basketball player in the history of the game, who simply recognized the need to give back to the community where he grew up: Akron, Ohio. He considered his own story, the eighty-three days he missed from school during his fourth-grade year, the disappointment and defeat in the eyes of his teachers when he was growing up, and decided that he would use his resources to create something beautiful for kids who find themselves in similar situations. The foundation started with community work, offering full college scholarships to students who met certain criteria, but quickly realized that it needed to do more if it wanted to make a significant impact. This is where the opportunity to combine threads of the spiderweb developed.

James reached out to his hometown's school district and was granted use of an old building, which he refurbished and reopened within a matter of weeks. The I Promise School, which opened in 2018, operates as a public school under the auspices of the district. However, in addition to the $2 million the district contributes toward the school's budget, James kicks in an additional $600,000 to fund extra teaching positions, after school activities, and tutors. The increased funding allows the school to keep the student-to-teacher ratio lower than other schools. There's also a laserlike focus on the parents and caregivers who send their students to I Promise. They are invited to come to the building during the school day to work on their GED or pick up food from the school's pantry.

Results are still preliminary, but the reading and math scores of the third and fourth graders enrolled at the school showed a significant increase, according to a 2019 *New York Times* article about the school. Since kids were targeted for participation because their test scores were at the absolute bottom of the scale, this step forward is cause for celebration. It's a sign that relationships are being built, confidence is being gained, and the community has bought in to the possibility of change that this experiment can birth.

This is what we need more of in this nation. We need smart, dedicated, strategic people with access to resources to inject innovation into schools that could do a better job of educating the most vulnerable citizens in our society. Egos have to be swept aside, and room has to be made for the best ideas. LeBron James came to the negotiating table with a famous name, a track record in the community, and the money to put ideas about improving education into practice. These factors paved the way for district officials to trust his foundation enough to enter into a partnership that is now benefiting the entire community. Other celebrities, seeing the obstacles faced by children living in low-income communities, have used their fame as leverage to create equally compelling platforms for change.

Let me be clear, I am not advocating that we swing wide the doors of the education system and invite every person with an idea to sit at the table and make decisions for millions of students. People who have no experience working with children, or who have spent little time attempting to understand the art and science of teaching, are the least qualified to lead schools. Some have argued that running a school system is no different than running a successful corporation. Set goals, work toward them, evaluate employees, measure progress. What gets left behind in this capitalist approach to education is the importance of building strong relationships, celebrating the strengths of children who have been historically disadvantaged, and communicating to families that they are valued. Many of the powerful elements of the Negro schools that existed before integration fall by the wayside when we think of educating our kids as just another business. When political and economic forces become more important than inspiration and creativity, we have lost our way.

The kind of collaboration I'm suggesting leaves the important decisions about progress and how to make things better for kids who struggle in the hands of educators who have a sense of what works. The partnership between Akron's school district and the LeBron James Family Foundation is a good example of how a citizen can call attention to a problem and work with the system to create a new solution.

International collaborations have also given rise to promising educational models. In 2000, Oprah Winfrey was inspired by Nelson Mandela, then president of South Africa, to open a school. The Oprah Winfrey Leadership Academy for Girls opened seven years later and has improved hundreds of lives since then. Winfrey said that she wanted to find girls that she thought reflected her own story, when she was young and intellectually gifted but living in poverty. In addition to the chance to get a good education, students live and study in luxurious accommodations and can understand how much they are valued. In 2019, Winfrey announced that she was considering opening a similar school in America.

Like James, Winfrey had the necessary tools to entice leaders to take her seriously and give her the room she needed to bring about a new reality in education. The school uses the curriculum sanctioned by the country's educational leaders. Within South Africa's parameters and educational standards, the school's faculty pursues divergent roads of development and intellectual growth. Many of the students have said that the school saved their lives.

Even when the collaboration is not inspired by a celebrity, it can be successful. Akbar Cook, a principal at the West Side High School in Newark, New Jersey, invited the world onto his campus through his appearances on the *Ellen DeGeneres Show* and other national television programs. Along with other innovations, Cook took the bold step of setting up a laundry room in his school so that students who were being bullied about wearing dirty clothes could wash a load before or after school. The response to this move on his part has been overwhelming. Privileged and wealthy people all over the country have stepped forward to purchase additional washing machines and dryers, laundry detergent, and other supplies needed to keep the program viable. During his first appearance on *Ellen*, Cook accepted a $50,000 check from Cheerios on behalf of the Lights On Program at West Side. An article on the show's website offers easy instructions for viewers to donate, mentor, volunteer, or sponsor the school and its programs.

Stories like James's, Winfrey's, and Cook's go a long way to inspire us. They allow us to pick up the paper or turn on the television and take comfort in the idea that good things are happening on the educational front. Collaborations are working. We applaud the efforts of these extraordinary people, seeing in them the drive and humanity we wish that others would demonstrate. Stories like these give us cover and on some level release us from our responsibility to get involved. We begin to think that you have to be famous to make a difference, or you must be a school official to make a difference. What we have to remember, though, is that every thread of the spiderweb is strong, and every thread is necessary. More than fifty million students attend public schools in America today. About fifteen percent of America's children live in households where the income falls below the federal poverty threshold. We need a sustained effort on a large scale to reach them. We need the public sector, the private sector, government entities, large corporations, unions, and the everyday average joe to take our children's education seriously and make fixing what's wrong our highest priority.

I may not boast the same level of name recognition or financial power as James or Winfrey, but I too felt an inspiration to create a space for the children we were leaving behind. Like the two of them, I could see where a change in our approach and an enhancement in the resources we offered could make a difference. But in 2012, when I approached the superintendent of the school district where I lived for help with adding a middle school Freedom Readers program to its successful kindergarten through fifth grade offering, the results were not the same. Perhaps if I had been a school principal like Akbar Cook, the conversation would have turned toward the collective, and some collaboration would have been possible. I was just the director of a nonprofit with a mere two-year track record and little hard data to add any credibility to the effort. Though the superintendent gave me a chance to explain our program, she showed little interest in working together to move it forward.

I was disappointed in that outcome, not only because I believed strongly in the plans for the middle school model, which was different from the K–5 approach, but because it felt like the children who had invested in the program were being short-changed and denied yet another opportunity. We'd said from the start that the goal of the K–5 program would be increased scores on standardized reading tests. Based on the information that parents shared with us, we could see improvement on that measure. However, I hoped for an official partnership between Freedom Readers and the school district, so that among other things, we could establish a data-sharing agreement that would help all area agencies and groups working on literacy see how the students progressed. When we approached the district with this idea, we were told repeatedly that the best way to collect the information was from the parents. School officials said that students knew their own reading scores, and could tell them to us if we only asked. We put a good bit of energy into collecting the data we needed from parents, but many of them had a hard time interpreting the data themselves. Some were simply not motivated to investigate Lexile scores, a measure of reading ability, and failed to respond to our request. A more organized system of analyzing scores and helping parents and caregivers understand their importance would have gone a long way.

We met with the superintendent to explain that our middle school program would help prepare students who had taken part in the K–5 program to achieve straight As on their report cards. We called it our International Baccalaureate (IB) Prep School, because we knew that high grades would put Freedom Readers scholars in a better position to apply for a spot in the prestigious IB program when they reached high school. Part of our goal was to make parents aware that they could petition to have their children placed in certain classes, even if no invitation had been extended by the school. As both a classroom teacher and an educational consultant working in urban school districts, I'd seen too many classes where the absence of students of color in IB, Advanced Placement, and other elite programs stunned me. I explained to the superintendent that I wanted to do something to address that disparity. Our middle school program would meet with scholars in the evenings and offer students a chance to work with experts in the four core subject areas they studied in school. We'd contact teachers to find out about assignments that were late or missing, one of the biggest problems middle schoolers faced. We'd have a table for each subject area, along with a table to help students get themselves organized and learn study habits. Our approach was a bit like AVID (Advancement via Individual Determination), the nonprofit program that helps high school students prepare for college that operated in our district and around the nation at the time. AVID targeted students whose grades were considered average, because its research indicated that students who have demonstrated potential would benefit most from its approach. We would focus on students living in low-income communities, many of whom were students of color. We felt that this emphasis would help mitigate some of the barriers to advancement that come with living in poverty or having to navigate a school in which systemic racism flourishes. In addition, we hoped to address the issues that were keeping students of color from enrolling and succeeding in the district's most challenging classes. While AVID was another programmatic addition to the school system, by operating outside the district, Freedom Readers was a move toward the abolishing of schools as we know them and starting fresh, without the bureaucratic constraints that impeded the progress of Black students.

Instead of embracing the ideas we shared, the superintendent said that the involvement of a group like ours was not needed: a great deal of money had been spent to pay the salaries of reading interventionists, who would work closely with any student who struggled with reading. Since my 2012 conversation with the superintendent, interventionists have been working hard, but test scores have barely budged. In 2018, Charleston's *Post & Courier* published an article with an alarming headline that spoke volumes: "South Carolina Spent $214 million on Child Literacy. It Didn't Work." The article described the problems with the South Carolina Read to Succeed Third Grade Retention Act, signed into law by Governor Nikki Haley in 2014. Read to Succeed was designed to respond to the South Carolina

Supreme Court's *Abbeville County School District v. South Carolina* decision, which mandated that the state "repair rampant funding inequalities between the state's richest and poorest districts." Lawmakers chose not to deal with the funding structure head-on, or even look closely at how poverty levels and racial segregation impact school. Instead, after two new state Supreme Court justices were appointed, the court voted to stop enforcing the decision just three years after it was made.

In this case, and far too often, the problem of failing schools was viewed through a political lens, making it difficult to ultimately make decisions that benefit children and enhance learning. This is not just happening in South Carolina. This pattern has been repeating itself for more than a decade, in states all over the nation. Republican governors like Jeb Bush warmly embrace legislation like the A+ Literacy Act, which calls for the retention of third graders if they do not meet certain benchmarks on standardized tests. By 2018, more than sixteen states had adopted similar bills.

It puzzles me that those charged with creating an education system that works effectively for all students would endorse a philosophy that punishes students who are not reading at grade level but at the same time reject approaches that could help those same children improve their reading skills. Research has shown that retaining children in a grade does little to help them achieve the desired goals, but does do measurable damage to their self-esteem and motivation. Retention has been linked to the ballooning dropout rate, and it comes as no surprise that it disproportionately impacts students of color. However, we live in a nation where some of our current leaders believe in the harsh and punitive treatment of those who struggle. Conservative voters and lawmakers wonder why children living in poverty can't just get themselves together. They argue that those children have had the same chances as other students to learn without taking into account the various barriers to success these children face. They don't think about the little girl who has had to deal with trauma and stress for so long that her brain has literally been reshaped by the flight-or-fight hormones coursing through her veins. They don't think about the dire situations in which children find themselves that are beyond their control.

Though I was unable to convince the district's leader that our work would be stronger together, we moved ahead anyway. We grew the K–5 program to eighteen locations and have been warmly embraced by local school principals. Our weekly meetings in those buildings are filled with the smiling faces of students the school believes would benefit most. We have grown the middle school program to two locations with the help of local principals and secretaries, who have helped us reach out to families in economically depressed communities. The reasons that a program like Freedom Readers is necessary becomes clearer with each child we meet. Not only do the results shine through in the confidence gained by the scholars, but we have come to more fully comprehend the role our volunteers play in making a difference on a broader level. Freedom Readers allows those of us who understand how students of color are disadvantaged within the education system to take a courageous step forward. Joining the ranks of our movement is by all rights an act of protest, a standing up to the forces that would paralyze young learners and shake their belief in their own potential. Meeting with young people each week communicates a strong resistance to the status quo. It calls attention to the inequities that exist by addressing them directly, through books and tutoring. In the same way that exercising our right to vote shores up our democracy, volunteering, especially to help young people in low-income communities read better, breathes life into our Constitution. All is not lost as long as we continue to struggle against oppression. As long as we insist that our thread of energy and encouragement and enrichment is added to the threads offered by the school district, there is hope. Together we can tie up the lion of underachievement and make the playing field more level.

The power of the collective is something Frederick Douglass understood better than most. Even while he was still enslaved, he went around the law, around the directives of the plantation owners, around what some considered to be the natural order of things, and secretly formed his own school. This oasis of joy and expectation was wrapped in the cloak of Christianity, the place where the enslavers trusted that they could gain a firm hold on the mind of the Black believer. Douglass organized a Sunday school where he was only to speak of the biblical passages that encouraged slaves to obey their masters. Instead, he used the opportunity to teach other enslaved people how to read:

> I held my Sabbath school at the house of a free colored man . . . I had at one time over forty scholars, and those

of the right sort, ardently desiring to learn. They were of all ages, though mostly men and women. I look back to those Sundays with an amount of pleasure not to be expressed. They were great days to my soul.

**After escaping** a life of enslavement, Douglass, a voracious reader of the Bible and a deeply spiritual soul, sought solace in the pews of the Methodist Church of Massachusetts. What he couldn't tolerate was the blatant segregation and racism that ran rampant within those very walls. The enslaved and free Blacks were forced to sit in the balcony, while others sat in pews closer to the pulpit. Even the sacraments were given to the different groups at different times. Grieved by these slights, Douglass turned his back on the mainstream Methodist Church and turned to the African Methodist Episcopal Zion Church. He became an ordained minister there, and continued to develop the oratorical expertise that would eventually make him what the Yale professor and Douglass biographer David Blight called the most famous Black man in the world and the most photographed person of his day.

In taking on that Sunday school, Douglass blazed a trail for the likes of LeBron James and Oprah Winfrey. It's safe to say that he was motivated by his own story, the days of hunger, the beatings he endured, the tattered clothes he was forced to wear when the weather was frigid. He held on to the memory of each encounter, the look on the faces of his siblings the last time he saw them, before they were separated and sold to different plantations. He also remembered a kind lady with white skin who taught him how to read. Her interest in him and teaching had a profound impact on his future. He remembered the words of his teacher's husband when he demanded she abandon the lessons because they would ruin young Frederick and make him forget his place. Every aspect of his literacy development was yet another prompt toward the day when he would stand before the forty scholars in his secret Sunday school, joyously sharing what he knew. In the absence of every conceivable advantage—he was as far away from a celebrity at that point as one could get and didn't have a penny to his name, and he didn't even legally own his own body—he presided over a school, seeking to uplift and empower. Eventually, the plantation owners discovered that he was teaching reading instead of the sanctioned Scriptures, and disbanded the meetings. But he never stopped heralding the virtues of literacy and how it could lift a man or woman out of bondage. He knew that the more of his brothers and sisters who were armed with knowledge, the better their chances would be of knowing freedom together, as a collective.

Douglass was motivated by his own experience, yet there must have been an even greater force compelling him: his belief in a higher power that would sustain him no matter what the situation. It is that indomitable spirit that kept alive many generations of the enslaved. It was both comfort and agitator, as it promised relief from trouble and rest on one hand and urged dramatic action on the other. This faith did not allow Douglass to merely accept his fate. It spoke of an obligation he had to his hurting family members long after he had gained his freedom.

In today's America, those of us who would have a positive impact on education can collaborate with existing structures such as school districts, but we must not turn a blind eye to the weaknesses that exist. We can raise our voices in support of the overlooked. We can connect with the places in a child's spirit that are eager to learn, grow, and reach new heights. We can stand with a child and family to let the world know that they are not fighting alone. And when we are successful, we will hear the voices of the next generation cry out to keep us all free.

# CHAPTER SEVEN

Historically, the two institutions in our society most impervious to change have been the church and the school. Both are built on ritual, leaning heavily on how things were done in the past and resisting ideas that might lead to radical shifts. Some of this resistance can be credited to people's desire to cling to tradition and some of it is simply because the institutions have grown so large that changing course requires a Herculean effort. In the case of the church, this reliance on yesterday's thinking and processes has resulted in the perpetuation of inequity and racial injustice. For schools, the result has been the same, but the reach has been even more harmful to families of color, who are required to send their children to schools that in many cases are not designed to meet their specific needs.

Despite this long-standing resistance to innovation, churches and schools alike have arrived at a crucial moment in their evolutions, one that will be seen by historians as nothing short of miraculous. As I write this, a virus is sweeping the nation, spreading more rapidly than anyone could have predicted, making it unsafe for large groups to gather in buildings for any reason, and thus threatening the existence of large institutions as we know them. For the first time in recent memory, churches and schools were ordered to shutter their doors by state governors all over the country. Along with multiple other sectors, churches and schools scrambled to move their business online, making use of technological platforms that enabled them to continue to operate. The results have been interesting, though the full impact will not be understood for years. However, we do know a few things about this quick transition. First, we must acknowledge that the change was made, enormous institutional ships turned almost in the opposite direction in just a matter of days. It's no small feat that millions of children across the country were provided with lessons and devices on which to complete them digitally, and millions of worshipers watched livestreams, participated in conference calls, and sat in church parking lots while preachers delivered their messages through loudspeakers and megaphones. The first thing we know is that although change is not easy, when necessary, churches and schools can adapt and re-create themselves to meet certain needs. The need, though, must be considered dire and pervasive enough for leaders to gather the political will to do it. We also know that there is a stark difference between churches gathering people online or on a call for a weekly service and schools attempting to finish out a school year with daily online lessons.

When many teachers were skeptical about the influence that some parents had on their children during a normal school year, the closing of public schools all across America put parents in the driver's seat. Because of physical distancing mandates, school officials no longer had direct access to learners after schools physically closed. Teachers could not monitor a child's behavior or offer consequences when a student did not comply with requests. Teachers could only provide the lessons. Parents had to be the ones to step up to see that they were completed in a timely manner, with some fidelity. Some parents relish the opportunity to spend more time with their kids, pulling them close and making sure that they take advantage of the slower pace of the family's days. These parents, mostly mothers, share gushing posts with friends on social media about the game nights their kids are enjoying, the time they spend running in the sun in the backyard, the family dinners they all enjoy. Reports like these are largely dispatched from the upper and upper-middle class, from the homes where parents have the type of job that allows them to work remotely. These are our nation's teachers, attorneys, bankers, writers. What dealing with a pandemic has taught us, though, is that the 70 percent of essential workers who do not have a college degree are working jobs with less flexibility and are feeling the brunt of the school shutdowns. The experience of cutting the school year short is vastly different in the households of these essential workers, not to mention the alarmingly high number of children who have not submitted any work at all since schools closed. Education leaders are beginning to wonder if the thousands of students who haven't been reached by teachers or administrators for a variety of reasons will be lost to public school systems forever.

Neither essential workers nor parents who work remotely have been able to successfully adjust to their new roles as classroom instructors. Even middle-class and affluent families have generally reported a sense of dissatisfaction with new home-school routines. Though some have decided to celebrate the silver linings described by the parents I mentioned earlier, most parents describe a deep sense of frustration in trying to meet the requirements of their online jobs while helping their children navigate their online lessons. A friend of mine, an elementary school administrator, told me that when her middle school son is supposed to be working on assignments sent to him by his teacher, he visits the gaming websites that genuinely pique his interest. Many parents find it difficult to keep track of what is really going on with their kids when they are planted in their chairs behind the computer screen. Caregivers are complaining of a sense of a fractured existence with an attention span of their own nearly depleted by the realities of a public health crisis raging all around them. Sleep patterns have been disrupted as adults and children alike feel as though their days are melding into one another.

When asked to describe the experience of trying to juggle their responsibility for their child's learning and their own work obligations, many caregivers use one word: stressed-out. The children themselves have been deeply impacted by school closures as well, but may not be as equipped to articulate their feelings. Children have lost their routines and rituals, the aspects of many of their young lives that helped them feel safe. Knowing what to expect from a day anchors many children, helping them to shift out of flight-or-fight mode into a space where they can learn new things. Without the structure that characterizes a school day, many students experience a heightened sense of anxiety, grief, and unease that manifests itself in their behavior. In addition, young children are wired to socialize with others through structured and unstructured play. Much of the preschool and primary grades curriculum is built around this human interaction, but with schools closed, playing with children outside the family unit is difficult for some and impossible for others.

Based on what I've heard through informal conversations, the youngest children, those in kindergarten through second grade, have been saddled with the most schoolwork. Educators across the board are dealing with a fear that children will miss a window of learning. This is especially true for kindergarten teachers, who help learners build important foundations in their formative years. This is when children are supposed to be learning to read and count on their own. Schools expect them to be able to recognize the letters of the alphabet and understand that the letters represent sounds, and units of sounds make words. Through their online lessons, teachers provide the basic skills while caregivers are tasked with overseeing the practice that is necessary to make these skills stick. While the lessons themselves may be well constructed, if teachers lack a firm grasp of the art and science of teaching online and how that approach is different from face-to-face classroom learning, students will not excel. As I acknowledged earlier, the fact that the change to online learning happened at all is to be celebrated, but it is also true that the speed with which the transition occurred may have led to a loss in quality instruction.

To say that schools were woefully unprepared for this would be unfair. Online learning has been a part of most school districts for years now, simply because educators recognized that many industries, along with just about every other part of our society, had moved online. Children have been sitting in front of screens during their leisure time for years, and educators have labeled them digital natives. So it's inaccurate to assume that schools have not incorporated computers into the fabric of their days. Furthermore, who could have predicted that we'd end up here, in a place where all we would have is technology to help us educate our children? This new reality was completely unexpected, and it's hard not to wonder what will happen to this generation of learners. What will be the impact of this time away from the trained professionals in the classroom?

It's not as if we haven't taken breaks from learning before. Where I live, schools are routinely closed when there is the threat of hurricanes or floods. We have even built an extended break into each school year. Researchers have long studied the effect of summer vacation, that time set aside in the educational calendar when schools go dark and families are forced to navigate the educational journey of young children. Towns like mine, which rely on strong summer tourist seasons to bring in tax dollars, have lobbied to keep summer vacation in place even when the research has shown that children lose a portion of what they had learned during the school year. This phenomenon has been termed "the summer slide," and like many detrimental educational realities, this slide has a greater impact on children from families of color. While affluent parents may require their children to continue to read and may take them on trips to museums and tours of overseas countries, many parents can't afford such luxuries. Caregivers living in low-income communities still need to work during the summer months. Often the most important aspect of summer for these families is finding a place where children can go and be safe while parents work. The highest quality summer camps can be extremely expensive, leaving children from low-income communities in camps that resemble day care centers, often staffed with employees who have little understanding of how children learn.

The concept of the summer slide may well apply to the new situation we are facing in America, where the last three months of the 2019–20 school year were effectively erased. Schools in most states reopened after Labor Day, with many choosing to provide instruction online or through a mix of in-person and online learning. Though schools did remain open for business in South Carolina, the very first weeks of online learning, in March 2020, were shaped by the state superintendent's mandate that teachers not introduce any new material. Students were to review material that they had learned previously and cement that learning through simple activities. For some students, this was a welcome chance to catch up with their peers if they had been falling behind. For those who had been excelling, this repeat of concepts felt like a punishment. When it became clear that the shutdown would last longer than a few weeks, though, the state superintendent and her advisers took another look at the way instruction was being handled. Teachers were asked to pivot and begin covering the predetermined learning goals for each grade level not previously addressed; standardized testing was canceled, and educators began to think of new ways to engage all their students.

It's too early to tell if the "shutdown slide" will be less or more significant than the summer slide we've been studying for decades. What we know so far is that teachers have approached online instruction in different ways simply because there are varying degrees of comfort with technology among educators. Many families are asking what they can do to keep students engaged in learning, to help them become truly invested and excited about broadening their minds instead of simply checking off tasks from a list. Short of finding ways to supplement the school-provided curriculum with board games that might teach math skills or reading together aloud, many parents are at a loss. If surveyed, I believe teachers, students, and parents alike would report that online learning is not what they signed up for. All of us are doing the best we can to make the most of a challenging situation.

It's going to be extremely important to remember the families like the ones served by Freedom Readers when we are able to safely gather again. Whatever the impact of the slide, it will hit them the hardest. Families living in small apartments in public housing will find it harder to focus on the educational needs of all their children when there are many. Parents who have to go to work at nursing homes and grocery stores may discover that it is almost impossible to obtain childcare because their day care center is closed; they will be stretched thin. Shutting down schools could not be avoided, but some children are being quarantined with their abusers, some are living with adults who are struggling with addiction, while others suffer from mental illness. The unemployment rate has skyrocketed, adding even more pressure to homes led by laid-off workers. These areas will need our attention more than others. And the need for the kind of education support we provide will extend beyond what we historically thought of as low-income communities. Living through a pandemic will undoubtedly cause parents all over the socioeconomic spectrum to wonder if they are doing enough to help their children excel academically.

Even as we struggle to find the right educational path for all students, we can learn valuable lessons from the successes that Freedom Readers experienced while we were still able to meet in person. Our victories have given us a chance to analyze the literature about what we can do to support children as they become expert readers and observe firsthand the impact of these practices outside school walls. Our ten-year track record of working with families has helped us gain a greater understanding of what works. It's possible to take what we've learned and incorporate new practices into our parenting and our work with children, especially children of color and those living in low-income communities. This shutdown of schools gives us the opportunity to rethink our approaches and perhaps reshape some areas of a system that was failing too many learners.

**Although there were multiple bends** in the road that seemed to lead to doors locked tightly against our progress, there have also been many triumphs for Freedom Readers over the last ten years. There were times when I was reminded of the goodness in people and their willingness to step forward on behalf of the vulnerable. Currently we sit at a crossroads in American history. Political polarization has taken over our discourse in every area, has reduced us to binaries and simplistic explanations of right and wrong. What is needed now is an emphasis on the core principles of humanity. Relationship, resilience, respect. My experiences with Freedom Readers have taught me that there are spaces of agreement and understanding that transcend difference, especially when it comes to vulnerable children. Opportunities for unification exist, but cultivating them the right way will be key. When we focus our energies in support of the future of the children who live in low-income communities, we all end up winning.

For instance, we have seen the test scores of children in our program soar. This is one of the most important measures of our work. Not only do we seek to justify to those who would invest their funds in our work that we are making progress toward our goals, but we also want to know for ourselves if the approaches we've embraced are really worth the time. After extensive conversations about how to acquire the quantitative data that would indicate success, we decided that since local schools and schools all over the country administer standardized tests on a regular basis, we should lean on those scores to help us track the growth of each scholar. In choosing this particular measure, we made it easier for our scholars to come to our program to engage in reading for a purpose, reading that reflects their choices, and reading that can be enjoyable, without the burden of further testing. Although we are thrilled to see the increase in standardized test scores, we realize that their true value is limited. These tests are but a brief, incomplete snapshot of what a student can do. They evaluate performance on a particular day under specialized conditions and leave out the external factors that impact a child's performance. If a child has had a fight with his parents the morning of the test or has stayed up half the night listening to his parents argue or shows up to school hungry, his performance will be impacted. Standardized testing administered on a laptop is different from a test given by a teacher with whom a child has developed a relationship. As an educator who finds great promise in what abolition could mean and look like in schools, I advocate for the defunding of standardized tests and favor an evaluation system that measures student growth instead of their test-taking ability and that utilizes culturally responsive teaching materials.

Not every child that crosses the threshold of our program comes with a built-in joy that leads them to pick up books and engage immediately. If that were the case, there would be no need for a program like ours. The Freedom Readers philosophy involves connecting with the children whose spark for reading has not yet been ignited, those children for whom reading translates to little more than decoding words or going through the motions of making sounds. We are here to serve all children, including the ones who might have been diagnosed with attention deficit hyperactivity disorder (ADHD), dyslexia, or other disorders that may keep them from experiencing reading success. We seek to offer an environment for all scholars that is enriching and overflowing with positivity and the kind of encouragement that calls out the best in children. As I've stated earlier, it's not our goal to replace the classroom teacher, but to support the work of the school in an environment that is deliberately absent of the distractions that make learning in a school setting virtually impossible for some youngsters. That means that we intend to assist young people as they advance from wherever they are on the spectrum of learning to the next point. With a constant eye toward the safety of all involved, every child is assigned an individual, trained tutor, making personalized learning a possibility.

Our largest group of scholars are the ones who have simply been bored by reading activities that might involve repetitive worksheets or exercises that fail to connect with their lived experiences. Though we draw heavily on the advice of special education professors and those trained in particular approaches to working with children with dyslexia, we aim to offer to every child the opportunity to attach happy memories with stories. We also draw on the work of researchers and scholars such as Gloria Ladson-Billings, Geneva Gay, and Lisa Delpit, all of whom offer great insight into what it takes to successfully inspire Black children and other children of color.

Ike and I started reading to our children before they were even born. We did our best to make sure that they knew our voices, and it seemed as if they understood the rhythms of stories at a very young age. Before they knew how to talk or even hold their heads up, we were reading more stories to them and asking them questions about those stories and pointing out pictures. These activities happen to be the cornerstone of learning to read. Researchers have discovered that the human brain is hardwired for language, and when young children are immersed in a word-rich environment their brains begin to form pathways or connections for which they are predisposed. The theory goes that the more words children hear when they are young, the more words they will be able to understand and vocalize when they start to talk. This leads to a deeper and better understanding of the concepts that children encounter in their reading lives as well.

What is sometimes left out of this discussion is how much the teaching of reading reflects the kind of reading and literacy practices that characterize middle-class homes, while leaving out any recognition of the value of experiences that take place in low-income communities. There are words, expressions, and linguistic patterns that make sense in certain neighborhoods that would feel out of place in others. Teachers who are successful in teaching students of color to read and comprehend on a high level have an understanding of both what is considered to be standard English and what might be the mother tongue of children living in low-income communities. The key is figuring out how to walk that line without passing judgment on the child's family or experience. The essential component of this work is trading a deficit model, which focuses on what the school system might say a child is missing, for a strength-based approach, which looks for what a child might know or do well. Taking a look at the culture in which a child is raised can shed a significant amount of light on where he or she might be gifted. Celebrating strength and showing respect for where a child begins can help tutors in the Freedom Readers program and teachers in the classroom build bridges of trust from what a child knows to what we know he or she needs to learn.

This is the reason that we so carefully craft our weekly meetings around themes that make sense to children and stimulate their curiosity. While classroom teachers are given a prescribed curriculum and asked to shape that teaching guide to fit the needs of the students in front of them, we have the flexibility of taking what we have learned about the needs of the scholars in our program and crafting a custom-built curriculum. Coupled with the opportunity to sit with one adult who has been trained in effective ways to share stories, this curriculum goes a long way in engaging the interests of the students, which we consider to be the first step in improving literacy skills. It may take a few weeks or even a few sessions, but the majority of children that come to us hating books and stories end up gravitating toward them when we figure out the right match of tutor and scholar. When the reading partnership is able to settle on the right book, that's when things start to change and we see progress. Scholars tend to want to read more when they are with us and when they are at home—after we connect them with the book that lights the spark. They come into the meetings with requests for more books by certain authors, and their eyes light up when they tell us about what they've read during the week. Sometimes it's a book they first discovered in school but did not have the time to finish. Sometimes it's a series of books that keeps them moving in the right direction. Whatever the case, this is the point where it feels like a flower has bloomed.

After a scholar has reached the point of becoming engaged, we are not surprised when they come to us with standardized test scores that have risen beyond the expectations of their teachers. We know that giving children an opportunity to practice, to choose, and build a reading relationship with a caring adult outside of their family leads to high test scores. Those higher scores often translate into better grades, which open up more doors of opportunity for children. It is this process that helps us address issues of unequal access to a good education.

For the caregivers reading this who are searching for concrete things that they can do to help their children read better at home, here are five ideas, all based on best practices as defined by educational research and what we've observed at our weekly meetings.

**Receive.** The first meetings of our Freedom Readers sessions are set aside for getting to know more about the learners with whom we are working. We encourage all caregivers to deliberately set aside time to find out more about the child's reading interest. Our interest inventory is reproduced in Appendix A. You can use these questions to help children begin to articulate their preferences and interests. Combine this knowledge with what you have noticed or observed about the child, and construct a personalized reading profile. The key is to say as little as possible and simply receive the information that many young children are more than willing to share. A few thoughtfully timed questions for clarification can go a long way, but for the most part, let the child lead.

**Research.** Find books that align with the reader's interest. If the child loves animals, scour the library for books about the specific animals that have been mentioned. You don't have to spend a fortune on these books. Drop by the local library and ask the librarian to help you check out the right book. Some of those books will spark the interest of the reader and some will fall flat. Explore a few different interests at one time, and notice which ones elicit the most intense reaction. Try fiction, nonfiction, comic books, picture books, poetry, and more. The key is to expose the reader to as much as possible while working within their zone of interest. Also, allow the young reader to choose what he wants to read in order to keep him engaged.

**Record.** Keep a list on the refrigerator of the books you and your child read together. Make a note of authors that seem to be the child's favorites and provide more of those books. If a child gravitates toward one series, try to find others like that one. If the books you suggest do not get a great response, browse through websites and let your child make suggestions. If her suggestions end up getting read most often, make a note of that as well. Check the appendix for a sample reading record list.

**Read aloud.** Even older children need to hear stories read by good readers. If you don't feel comfortable doing the reading, in the appendix there is a list of websites you can check that will do the reading for you. Allow children to read out loud to you so that you can get a sense of their ability to decode words.

**Respond.** Reading is a social act. Share with the young reader connections that the stories bring to mind. Help relate what you are reading to the real world and to the reader's experience. Praise young readers who use the skills they are learning in school to figure out the pronunciation of new words instead of telling them the words right away. Always point out what the reader is doing well and explain that the brain is like a muscle. It grows stronger as we exercise it.

We've found these basic principles lead to success with many of our scholars. As we transition back to a time when we can gather safely, we'll continue to incorporate these principles into our online offerings. As many caregivers find ways to support their child's reading development, these strategies will take on new meaning. Don't forget that consistency is important, and routines matter.

# CHAPTER EIGHT

As I write this it feels a bit like the world is coming apart at the seams. I'm at my desk in my office as usual. I can see the sun coming up behind the trees to greet me, as birds outside my window sing another day into existence, but nothing is the same as it was when I started writing this book. It's the first week of May 2020, and we've been in self-isolation for seven weeks, working hard to keep ourselves and our neighbors safe, doing what we can to stop the spread of COVID-19, the infectious and deadly virus that has claimed almost 270,000 lives worldwide.

The death toll is staggering, almost too much to comprehend. I hesitate to even write about it for fear that I will somehow dishonor the realities of those who have been most directly affected. There have been moments when I have felt as if I'm stuck in some weird science fiction movie where the cure is just beyond our reach. There are moments when I sit and think about the families who are grieving loved ones, and it's almost too much to take. The entire planet is processing a collective trauma right now. Be it through our dream life or conscious mind, we are all trying to make sense of something that was once unimaginable, a freight train barreling down on us. And we never even saw it coming.

And in the middle of this strange new reality, Freedom Readers celebrates a significant anniversary, our tenth. What we thought was going to be a day of reunion, champagne toasts, and warm embraces turned out to be another day in isolation. Another day that we won't see our scholars or their tutors, another day of grim news. But somehow life inches forward, and milestones roll around and you have to make a choice: collapse under the weight of the circumstances or get up and fight. On May 4, 2020, I chose the latter.

When we got the word in late March that schools were closing, the board of directors and I had already made the decision to suspend our weekly meetings. Many of our volunteers are senior citizens, and we were being told at the time they were the most vulnerable to the disease's effects. We thought about how children often get colds in the spring and give little thought to how germs spread. We moved quickly to try to protect everyone involved. The decision, however, was not an easy one. It broke my heart to think about all that we'd planned for 2020. In January we adopted a new guiding principle: 2020 2.0. There was a strategy in place to step up our efforts in every area and become a stronger, better, faster version of ourselves. At our annual board retreat in January we adopted our most ambitious budget to date, incorporating all of the new relationships we intended to build with local organizations and businesses, as well as money for essential staff who had volunteered their time up to that point. The anchor of our new budget was our relationship with foundations in our area, including the Chapin Foundation and the United Way. Historically, these have been our largest sources of income, and we were poised to request even more support on the strength of our track record. Everything seemed to be moving in the right direction until the virus that the president of the United States said in late February would be "a little like a regular flu" started claiming lives on American soil at a rate that we've never seen. For Freedom Readers, it was like driving into a brick wall at a hundred miles per hour, only you are watching it unfold in your mind in slow motion. And there is nothing you can do about it.

This feeling of impending doom, this sense of crumbling in on yourself, is not unique to Freedom Readers. The worldwide economy feels like it's running down the street naked, with its hair on fire. In many areas restaurants were closed, because staying six feet away from others while enjoying a meal is virtually impossible. This set off a domino effect, with consequences that rippled out for miles. Beyond the obvious layoffs of waitstaff, cooks, and hostesses, food that would have been consumed inside those restaurants wasn't bought, and went into the trash, hurting the grocery stores, food manufacturers, and farmers' bottom line. When the farmers aren't getting paid for the harvest, they have less money to invest in planting and hiring workers to keep the farm going. Imagine this scenario playing itself out repeatedly in just about any business sector you can think of. The ripples keep getting bigger and wider, until every person on the planet is touched.

I keep hearing the phrase "We're all in this together." I guess this mantra is supposed to bring us comfort, and in some ways it does. Though our knowledge of how the virus is transmitted has improved, the sense of uncertainty surrounding this public health situation has not. When we scratch the surface, it's easy to see that there are differences in the way this current crisis is hitting different demographics. Those who were struggling and vulnerable before this happened, such as many of the families served by Freedom Readers, are seeing an even greater tidal wave of grief and despair. Now that the middle class and the wealthy are at risk as well, the nation is forced to confront issues of income inequality and racial injustice in new ways. The virus has sharpened our national vision.

Nonprofit organizations, the ones designed to reach people in need and provide for them in ways that our government cannot or will not, are being hit especially hard by this new and insidious trickle-down economics. Though nonprofits like ours have always been on the front lines of the battle, some lawmakers have been waging war against the poor, and we've also been undervalued and taken for granted. In the ten years that I have been a nonprofit leader, I've received dozens of awards, have been the focus of several news reports, and have even been lauded in speeches by the same school superintendents and housing authority leaders who fight me tooth and nail behind closed doors. But when it comes to offering the funding needed to keep operations running smoothly, the support is less enthusiastic. Small, rural nonprofits like Freedom Readers rely on public financial support to help us do our work. There are rent payments and insurance bills and printing costs to think about, because nonprofits are businesses. We exist to serve the public good, yes, but at the end of the day the numbers have to add up, the books have to balance.

So when the foundations we rely on to help us advance our missions are no longer receiving revenue from the businesses that make tax-deductible contributions to them, we find ourselves between a rock and a hard place. The demand for our services increases exponentially, while the funding for our work decreases at a comparable rate. It's almost impossible to know how to take the next step without causing the house of cards to collapse all around you.

It shook me up when I realized that we had to suspend our spring session. My first thought was that it would be a short hiatus, much like the patterns we follow when we face the threat of severe hurricanes or extreme flooding. We were about seven weeks into an eleven-week session in which scholars and tutors were studying inventors and conceptualizing their own inventions. The break was painful yet manageable in my mind when

I thought that we'd just chill out for a few weeks and return in the summer. About three weeks into the self-quarantine period I received an email from our board treasurer: "I know it sounds like I'm ringing the alarms bells and I am. I've been watching the non-profit landscape around the state and employees are being furloughed. The short term is one thing, but we also have to think about the long-term health of this organization. Will there even be a Freedom Readers when this is over?"

Sometimes you need an objective career banker and economist to reach out of an email and shake you by the shoulders. I couldn't have been more startled than if he had poured cold water over my head in the middle of the night. I had been in denial about the toll the virus could take on Freedom Readers, maybe because I had been too close for too long. I had invested so much and saw our trajectory as always ascending. I was still in the 2020 2.0 mindset, when I should have already switched to crisis management mode. I'll be forever grateful for Jon Greenlee's willingness to tell it like it is.

After speaking with Jon and Jamia Richmond, our board chair, we decided that five of the organization's employees would be furloughed to protect the less than $100,000 we had in the bank at the time. Salaries are our biggest expense, and we had to make our money stretch to get us to the other side of the shutdown. At the same time, we knew that if we didn't figure out a way to remain relevant and active, none of our funders would be willing to continue funding us. Essentially, there would be nothing to fund.

I faced the task that no employer wants to face, nonprofit or otherwise. I had to be the one to pick up the phone and tell two full-time and three part-time employees that they were being laid off. Although I knew that the exact scenario was playing itself out in a million ways a million times over the country, that thought didn't make it any easier, didn't make me feel any better about what I had to say. I felt responsible. I was the one who had started the whole thing and who wouldn't stop pushing until it grew to a size that I couldn't manage on my own anymore. If I had just settled for working with the original groups at Darden Terrace and Huckabee Heights, I would not have needed to hire employees, and then I wouldn't be having to make those tough calls. I blamed myself.

Though I wallowed in long moments of self-pity and doubt, I fully understand that the funding issues that nonprofits face are much bigger than mine, or those of any single nonprofit leader. For instance, if our work is valued, why is our funding so unstable and unreliable? Completing grant applications was something I knew absolutely nothing about when I started this work. I had to figure things out quickly, research grant writing, try to get my hands on grants others had submitted that were successful, and figure out exactly what the funders wanted to hear, the buzzwords that made them feel warm and fuzzy. There were many rejections in the early days. In fact, my applications are still rejected on a regular basis. However, I've learned a great deal through trial and error. Many skeptical funders, influenced by horror stories of misappropriated funds, don't trust nonprofit leaders enough to support general operations with unrestricted dollars, and they don't want to pay for salaries. Most will agree to fund a request to purchase books, but others put so many restrictions on where and how funds can be spent that organizations often find themselves tied in knots. It goes back to the cloud of cynicism and suspicion that has lingered over the entire sector for generations. It can feel as if our communities want us to deal with poverty, homelessness, and low literacy skills, but they don't exactly trust us to know how to get it done effectively. Submitting these applications is like playing the lottery. If the reader is in a good mood that day, you might get the response you're seeking. But if you haven't been initiated into the language and atmosphere of what grant reviewers are expecting, you might as well hang it up. You'll probably get a no.

I'm not denying that some of that cynicism is healthy. Some money granted to nonprofits is misused, but that's also the case in the for-profit sector. White-collar crime is by no means exclusive to charities. It's always a good idea to vet organizations before investing, but don't let the actions of a few unscrupulous leaders negatively impact every nonprofit under the sun. Instead, why not seek ways to build capacity in small nonprofits so that the oversight necessary to ensure above-board operations are in place? Perhaps a stronger financial investment in community organizations could ultimately reduce the need to call police officers to situations for which they are unprepared and untrained. Maybe this approach could help us save lives.

Leaders of color hear that *no* much more than their white counterparts. A 2008 study of the foundation grants awarded to nonprofits that was conducted by the Greenlining Institute revealed that in 2005 only about 12 percent of national foundation grants went to organizations led by people of color. The well-known and respected Bill and Melinda Gates Foundation awarded only 10 percent of its dollars to minority-led organizations. What this report and others like it illuminate is a quiet racism that runs through the world of philanthropy just as it has in housing, education, and the criminal justice system. Minority-led nonprofits have historically been redlined in this country and set up to fail. This partially explains the fact that while I have been able to develop relationships with local foundations, the door to large, multiyear grants has remained locked and largely out of reach. Though I fully understand that I am not automatically entitled to financial support and no one owes me anything, the families we serve deserve the chances we provide. So I'm committed to making our program better and to knocking on every door.

Just this week I was able to secure a Payroll Protection Program forgivable loan from the federal government, which allowed me to bring our employees back for eight weeks. This will be the first time in ten years that we've received any federal funding. I know that the money exists, but sometimes I just don't know where it's hiding or how to get to it. It's not like there is a directory of funding you can check out of the library. Even if such a thing did exist, many funders will only work with organizations that they approach and have invited. Others simply will not bet on an unknown.

A weight has been lifted off my shoulders for the short term, but what happens when that money runs out? At least restaurants have a chance to start making more money when the government allows them to open fully and the general public decides it's safe to start eating out again. But when will the foundations we counted on be viable enough to fund us at the level where we were before the pandemic? How long will it take the nonprofit sector to recover? How many of us small, rural nonprofits won't make it to the other side?

Even though it feels like the world is coming apart at the seams as I write this, I'm also anchored in a reflective space of consciousness, an intellectual space that anniversaries and milestones often take me to. I can't help but think about the first days of Freedom Readers, when I was running on little more than adrenaline and a dream. The country was in the middle of a recession, industries were being bailed out, and the way forward was uncertain. I managed to connect with the executive director of a local foundation, who listened to my pitch for this new literacy thing I wanted to try. During our initial breakfast meeting, she leaned across the table and asked in her Paula Deen accent, "Don't you think we already have enough nonprofits?" She was right to point out the very crowded landscape of organizations waving the charity flag. Right now there are 1.5 million registered nonprofits in the U.S., and each one is seeking financial support. At some point, nonprofit leaders adopt a bit of a "survival of the fittest" mentality, while funders develop a sense of fatigue and a high degree of distrust. No matter how strong the program or how glamorous the promotional materials, donors choose the winners and losers in the nonprofit game.

In 2010, it wasn't guaranteed that Freedom Readers would end up on the winning side. I didn't exactly fit the profile of a business leader of any type. The various aspects of my identity—my womanhood, my Blackness, my southern heritage, my abolitionist/disrupter spirit—play a major role in how I see the world and how the world sees me.

Here again are the echoes of Du Bois's concept of double consciousness. I was determined to address an issue that I saw as important and critical. My family and I were prepared to go to great lengths to create an organization that would have a real impact and be scalable. That's how I saw myself. But there were others who viewed me as uninitiated, naive, overzealous, too young, too soft-spoken, too arrogant, and too proud. Was our gentrified nonprofit ecosystem ready for a thirty-something African American female leader? Would I be accepted or approved by the people I thought I could help, or the people who had the means to help me? Furthermore, according to the Small Business Administration Office of Advocacy, my odds were not great, since only half of all new businesses make it past the first five years. In my case, the learning curve was steep. There were articles of incorporation to file with the South Carolina Secretary of State. I needed a lawyer for that, and money to pay them. Then there was the application for a 501(c)(3) tax-exempt designation from the Internal Revenue

Service. I needed an accountant for that. I had no idea how to get any of this done, but I wasn't afraid to ask questions of the people I thought would have the answers. Fortunately, I had made friends over the years with a few high-profile movers and shakers. Chief among them was Sally Hare, the now-retired dean of education at the local university. Those of us who know and love her call her "the great connector." Were it not for Sally's willingness to patiently listen to all my questions and introduce me to the influential people in her network, I don't think our seed would have grown at all.

I've learned that starting, sustaining, and scaling a viable business of any type is about access. It's about being able to connect with the right people and hoping against hope that you can convince them that you and your idea are worth betting on. No matter how charismatic a leader might be, the program, company, restaurant, or school will fall flat on its face without the right kind of support. When you are an African American woman with a limited sphere of influence, it means everything in the world when a well-respected white person in a position of power steps forward and vouches for you. After I shared my idea with her, Sally would periodically take me to lunch and rattle off a list of names of folks at local foundations and elsewhere. She'd follow up with an email to me and the person she thought could help me, inviting us to keep the connection going. I jumped at every opportunity and was able to secure our first $10,000 grant through one of those contacts. Another one of those acquaintances put me in touch with a law firm that agreed to file the articles of incorporation for us pro bono.

Someone I met through Ike's newspaper column agreed to file the tax-exempt application with the IRS for free.

Lack of access to the right networks of support can lead to the death of many worthy organizations with outstanding potential, both in the start-up phase and at a time like this. One of the most frustrating things about leading an organization like Freedom Readers is what I refer to as the Sisyphus Effect, the act of pushing the financial boulder up the mountain only to see it roll back down again at the end of each year, when our budgets reset and we start over. It's emotionally exhausting to put so much of your heart and soul into a cause, one that is personal and urgent and critical, and see all the gains you made over the span of years slip through your fingers like grains of sand. Just when you think you have a little wind at your back and you think about starting to exhale for a moment, the wind shifts and you're right back at the bottom of the mountain again, trying to push that same rock. Only it's twice as heavy this time, because it's gathered more dirt as it rolls. It's like trying to get a pool of water in a headlock. And when your close network generally consists of people with limited disposable income, you are at the mercy of the well-connected and well-off.

On behalf of all nonprofits who are working in the low-income communities that have been disproportionately impacted by COVID-19 and the systemic racism it illuminates, I call on our local and federal legislatures to rethink the way they allocate our tax dollars. When police brutality rages out of control, it's time to think about spending that money in different ways. Give more to organizations that can deal with issues of mental health and conflict resolution, employment and education. Take organizations like Freedom Readers seriously. Stop taking for granted the studies that show that the work of community groups like ours can bring down the crime, gun violence, and gang activity rate, as residents in the community experience a sense of pride and become invested in the success of the children. Stop pouring so much money in the building of jails and prisons and focus on keeping young people from getting caught up in the justice system in the first place. Make sure nonprofits that are doing good work in these communities have everything they need. Underscore the reality that our nation will be judged by the way it treats the vulnerable. Strengthening them strengthens us all. Increasing access to a good education bolsters our young people, who have stepped forward to lead us even now. They are indeed our only hope for a better tomorrow.

**Those of us** who will emerge from this crisis with our health and our jobs will wonder what we can do help strengthen our community. We can remember those who have been impacted the most. We can remember organizations like the local homeless shelter and food bank, which help address the immediate needs of people who lose jobs and find themselves struggling, maybe for the first time. We can make donations, but we can also get to know the organization's leader and make that key introduction. We can talk to friends about supporting the causes that matter. We can share our networks and vouch for that leader of color or that organization trying to help communities of color, which have been hit hardest by the coronavirus.

When I started writing this book, I had firm ideas in mind about the next chapter for Freedom Readers. There would be programs for parents and caregivers to include mindfulness, education on the antidotes to childhood trauma and toxic stress, with a focus on nutrition, proper sleep, mental health care, and exercise. We'd invest in writing curricula that fills in the gaps in what is being taught in our history classrooms about people of color. We'd provide opportunities for children to publish their own books and hold readings and book signings. We'd get girls excited about STEM and coding through partnerships with local academies. There would be continued conversations with tutors and the community about issue of diversity, equity, and inclusion. And we would develop literacy programs for infants, middle schoolers, and high school students to complement our current work. When 2020 dawned I was once again running on adrenaline and a dream. But now, moving forward is an exercise in feeling our way through the dark.

**The word of the day** at Freedom Readers and around the world is "pivot." We've come to the point where we are all forced to let go of the idea that things will go back to the way they used to be before the pandemic. Embracing a new reality can be difficult, but when you realize that there is no other choice, you adapt. You pump up the volume of the wealth of resilience and creativity passed down to you by marginalized and oppressed forerunners. You wear the mask, but you don't stop smiling behind it. Even if the world can only see the smile in your eyes.

Our pivot rests on a new service we are calling the Reading Lab by Freedom Readers, which was inspired by the news that more than ten thousand children in our state had no contact with state-sponsored school districts during the entire five months that school buildings were closed. This number boggles the mind. What happened to all of those children? What is going to happen to our society if we don't reach them?

To make our services more accessible, we have torn down the walls of the program to welcome families at any time of the year, not just at the beginning of a ten-week session. Instead of offering weekly meetings, we offer appointments for a caregiver and a child to begin with an initial visit to the Reading Lab, where they will meet with a professional educator and a member of the Freedom Readers staff. Reading level is assessed, an interest inventory is administered, and the child will be allowed to choose a book from a group of five. These data inform the discussion that follows, which centers around the caregiver's concerns and questions. Immediately following the initial visit, caregivers are sent a reading prescription with recommendations for what families can do at home to strengthen reading skills. A follow-up visit with the team is scheduled for eight weeks out, and a tutor is assigned if requested.

Much of this work takes place over online platforms, but some still happens in small groups, with social distancing. So far we've assessed eleven children and have a total of about sixty-five on a waiting list. The education department at Horry-Georgetown Technical College is partnering with us to provide sixty tutors, who will work with us for course credit. One of our new tutors read about the opportunity on Facebook and reached out to us from Boston. She'll be working with a bilingual student in Myrtle Beach.

We've had the South Carolina Department of Juvenile Justice reach out to us about a fifteen-year-old girl who had been given community service as a punishment. In the course of her evaluation, she admitted that she could not read. The judge reduced her community service by half and ordered her to spend the remainder of the time receiving reading instruction. Her initial visit to the Reading Lab is scheduled for next week.

The potential to make a difference is real. The sparkle in the eyes of our children has not been extinguished. Hope is still springing high, and now is not the time to retreat. Now is the time to push. The story that follows describes what pushing looks like in my world these days, and the reasons that I just can't give up now.

**When I pulled** into the parking lot of the brick Baptist church on a warm afternoon earlier this week, they were already there waiting for me. As I approached them, the twins turned their masked brown faces my way. Their eyes danced, told me they were smiling and welcoming me though I was a stranger. Their team leader introduced us as I joined them under the aluminum shed. They sat in folding chairs. I sat behind a small folding table with my bags, folders, and books. We were ready to begin.

The nine-year-old twins were preparing to begin third grade. I called the brother over first and explained that I would ask him to read a story aloud and then retell what he could remember. I could tell that he was eager to show me what he could do. He placed his finger beneath each word and filled the air with the music of his strong voice. It rose and fell in perfect rhythm with the story's meaning. His comprehension skills matched his level of fluency. I smiled and told him he'd done a good job.

As a slight breeze tickled the back of my neck, I asked him about his interests, his favorite color, video game, TV show, person. I took notes as he talked about the kind of books he liked: books about sports and geography, nonfiction. He wants to be a police officer when he is older.

Finally, I showed him five books and asked him to choose the one that was best for him. *Reptiles* was the title he selected. I sent him home with it and made mental notes about the four books we would mail to him later. At least one book each week is what we expect him to read for the next eight weeks.

I would repeat that sequence four more times before taking the hour drive home. I met moms, grandparents, and aunties, some on their lunch break, some surprised to see me. "When they said Dr. Bailey, I pictured somebody entirely different!" I was told this by a beautiful widow with a flair for the dramatic.

On the way home I reflected on the significance of what I'd just experienced. I was sweaty, exhausted, and absolutely exhilarated all at once. Then my mind drifted to a more somber, reverent place. I realized that as much as that visit was for the benefit of the twins and their fellow scholars, it was meant to honor those whose lives were cut short before they could reach their full potential. In that moment, right there in my car, I dedicated the work to the memory of Tamir Rice, who should be getting ready for his first year of college, Trayvon Martin, Michael Brown, Ahmaud Arbery, George Floyd, and Breonna Taylor. We turn the pages of the books they can't hold, we dream the dreams they can't chase, we raise the torches they can't carry, and we protect the children here with us now. We do this work to block out the possibility of needing another hashtag. Not on our watch.

# CONCLUSION

On a snowy, bitterly cold January morning in 2014, I stood in the hallway of Mount Auburn Hospital in Cambridge, Massachusetts, watching my husband die. At least that's the way it looked to me. A very congenial nurse had just found the vein that would connect him to what we thought was a life-saving drug, intravenous immunoglobulin or IVIG. His headphones were in. "Purple Rain" pulsed through his brain almost loudly enough for me to hear it in the hallway as he squeezed his eyes shut. Prince was his go-to when it came to needles. This college-football-scholarship-earning man of mine needed something to help him keep his mind off the pain. There was nothing in the world that could distract me from the anxiety that threatened to overtake me, the fear that I would lose him, the calculus involved in figuring out how I was going to raise our two children alone if it came to that.

I watched him from the hallway because I didn't want him to see me cry. I needed to be strong for him. I wasn't the one who had been diagnosed with a life-threatening disease four weeks earlier. CIDP. Chronic inflammatory demyelinating poly-neuropathy. Neither of us had ever heard of it before. We just knew that he kept getting weaker by the day. Climbing stairs was becoming difficult. I looked up one morning while he was getting dressed and noticed for the first time that his flesh was looser than it used to be, soft where bulging muscles were once prominent. He was wasting away right in front of my eyes.

It was Ike who had to live through the rapid changes in his body, so he was entitled to feel a wide range of emotions. It was my job to do one thing. Stay strong. Hold it together. Be the rock. Hold his hand while he shed tears and described each new symptom that he noticed but couldn't explain. It was the heaviest weight I'd ever tried to carry in my life.

After having visited our family doctor, a chiropractor, and a podiatrist, we finally ended up in the office of Dr. Oscar Soto, a Boston-based neurologist who turned out to be one of the few doctors in the country that had ever diagnosed and success-fully treated CIDP. Things might have gone another way if we hadn't been at Harvard that year for Ike's Nieman Fellowship for journalism. It was one of those moments when we received exactly what we needed, at the exact time we needed it.

Over the course of the years that I have led the Freedom Readers organization, there have been a multitude of moments just like that. Grants that were due the day after we heard about them. People with just the experience we needed calling to volunteer when we needed that specific kind of help. I could not have orchestrated those happenings. They seemed to be laid out before me all the time, but I couldn't see around the corners. I just had to have the faith to take the next step on the journey.

Finding Dr. Soto was the blessing. Being hours away from my home and my family while trying to handle one of the most terrifying episodes of my life was the curse. I missed the Carolina sunshine, the warm breezes, my mama's bread pudding. I missed Freedom Readers most of all, because since its inception three years earlier, it had been like my third baby. I had given it my all, had stood up to the naysayers and the odds stacked against me to start an organization that could open doors of prosperity by helping kids fall in love with reading. Ike and I had spent hours talking about it and strategizing. We'd invested what little extra money we had into purchasing materials, and I had received no monetary compensation for my work in the beginning. We had no idea he'd be selected for the Nieman, one of the most prestigious journalism fellowships in the world. When he told me that we had been invited to Harvard shortly after I finished my doctoral program, I was elated. We'd get to sit in the Harvard library and breathe the air that swirled around W. E. B. Du Bois and Barack Obama when they studied there. It wasn't long before my elation gave way to trepidation.

What would happen if I stepped away from Freedom Readers? Would it survive without me?

I'm pleased to say that it not only survived, but in many ways it thrived. I called on a team of strong volunteers to take my place for a year. Sunny Fry stepped up to be interim director. She was supported by Bobbi Scofield, Jamia Richmond, Sandy Jackson, and a host of other folks, including our board of directors. They proved what many of my funders had wondered out loud: that Freedom Readers could continue to exist without my leadership, and that it wasn't just propped up by my passion and personality. That was an amazing blessing. Still, my husband wrestled with a rare and little-known disease that came out of nowhere and attacked him with a vengeance. CIDP caused his body to turn on itself and made his nerves stop communicating with his muscles. It was the curse that hung over us like a black cloud almost the entire time we were away.

I didn't know it at the time, but I was seeing firsthand the negative impact that adverse childhood experiences (ACEs) could have on the human body. As explained on the U.S. government's site Child Welfare Information Gateway, ACEs are traumatic events occurring before age eighteen. They include all types of abuse and neglect as well as parental mental illness, substance use, divorce, incarceration, and domestic violence. A landmark study in the 1990s found a significant relationship between the number of ACEs a person has experienced and a variety of negative outcomes in adulthood, including poor physical and mental health, substance abuse, and risky behaviors.

When Ike wasn't at a doctor's appointment or receiving treatments at the hospital, he went to classes, where he learned about ACEs. He was excited to tell me about this area of research because it could explain why a man who ran five miles a day, never smoked, never took a drink of alcohol, and ate a relatively healthy diet would get so sick so fast. We reasoned that it was part genetics and part childhood trauma. Though knowing a possible cause for our situation didn't make the curse seem any less potent, it did lead us to ask questions about what he could do about it and how we could intercede in the lives of children experiencing ACEs back home.

That investigation led both of us to the office of Jack Shonkoff, MD, a pediatrician and founding director of the Center on the Developing Child at Harvard. When I told Dr. Jack about Freedom Readers and how we hoped to make kids' lives better through reading, he congratulated me on my efforts and told me a little about his work. Since 2006 the Center's mission, as stated on its website, has been to "generate, translate, and apply scientific knowledge that would close the gap between what we know and what we do to improve the lives of children facing adversity." I knew that I had arrived at just the right place at just the right time. Our visions lined up perfectly.

And then he shared with me one of the most important lessons he'd learned over the years. Strong, stable relationships are key, chief among them being the relationship between the child and the caregiver, but even beyond that. The more caring adults a child has in his life, the more resilient he is likely to be, the better able he will be to cope with and counteract ACEs.

In essence, he was telling me that the best thing I could do for the children in the program I designed was continuing to connect them with trained tutors who they could count on to care.

I have carried that advice with me a long time. I have thought about it when dealing with my own children and especially in supporting my husband in the years since leaving Boston and moving back home. He did not die the day I stood watching him from the hallway with tears in my eyes. Despite spending more than a week in a Mount Auburn Hospital bed, having me push him around in a wheelchair and give him daily injections after he was released, despite fighting an incredibly high fever that would not respond to treatment, he survived. In the six years that have passed since that day, he has gained strength in every area. Not only has he survived, he has thrived.

I thought about Dr. Jack's advice when I returned to Freedom Readers, which survived as well. When I couldn't see around the corners, I feared I would never return. When Ike was at his weakest and he needed my help buttoning a shirt or tying his own shoes, I made sure my teaching certificate was current and contemplated applying to be a teacher in the local school district where I started my career. I did apply for a teaching job at virtually every college and university in South Carolina and never received so much as an interview. Panic threatened to take over, but I took each step before me by faith.

When I returned as CEO at Freedom Readers in the summer of 2014, I led the organization with a renewed fire for change and an understanding that we can be strengthened by hardship. That fire has propelled me and the organization through ten years of turnover, surprises, triumphs, and celebrations. There have also been disappointments, miscalculations, outright failures, broken promises, and wounds that took a long time to heal. But I had watched my husband dance with a disease brought on by circumstances beyond his control. Circumstances that many of the children enrolled in our program faced. I had seen my own biological children adapt to a new environment and a stressful situation with courage. Their resilience inspires me even to this day. And I could see that even though I only pretended to be strong when I stood in the hospital's hallway, I had genuinely started to grow into myself. There was a strength beneath the surface I didn't know existed that fortified me to rise up to meet whatever challenge lay just around the corner. I received that strength exactly when I needed it. Or maybe it was there all the time.

# FREEDOM READERS INTEREST INVENTORY

## SCHOOL

How old are you? _____

What grade are you in? _____

What is your favorite school subject? _____

What is your least favorite part of the school day?

_____

## HOME

Who lives in your home?_____
_____

What do you like to do at home?
_____

What do you like to do with your family? _____

I enjoy these types of reading:
(circle those that apply)

Storybooks      Magazines
Fiction         Fairy Tales
Nonfiction      Geography
Comics          Sports

## MY FAVORITE . . .

COLOR _____

TV SHOW_____

FOOD _____

RESTAURANT _____

PERSON _____

SINGER/RAPPER _____

VIDEO GAME _____

SPORTS TEAM _____

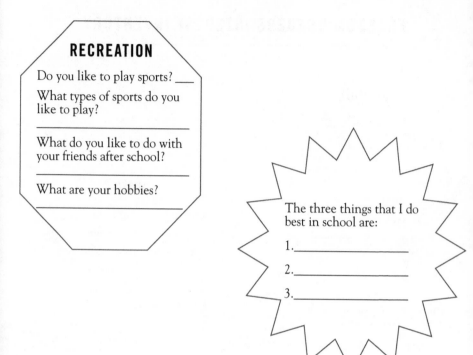

### RECREATION

Do you like to play sports? ___

What types of sports do you like to play?
_____

What do you like to do with your friends after school?
_____

What are your hobbies?
_____

The three things that I do best in school are:

1._____

2._____

3._____

## MY GOALS:

Some of the things that I would like to work on this year are:
_____
_____
_____

I would like to learn more about:
_____
_____
_____

In 10–15 years, I see myself:
_____
_____
_____

# READING RECORD

---

**STUDENT NAME:**

**AGE:**

**GRADE:**

**READING LEVEL:**

**GOAL (NUMBER OF BOOKS READ IN SUMMER):**

---

| BOOK TITLE | AUTHOR | NOTES |
| --- | --- | --- |
| | | |
| | | |
| | | |
| | | |
| | | |
| | | |
| | | |
| | | |
| | | |
| | | |
| | | |
| | | |
| | | |
| | | |
| | | |
| | | |
| | | |
| | | |

# WEBSITES FOR READ ALOUDS

### Storline Online
www.storylineonline.net
"The SAG-AFTRA Foundation's Daytime Emmy-nominated and award-winning children's literacy website Storyline Online streams videos featuring celebrated actors reading children's books alongside creatively produced illustrations."

### The Indianapolis Public Library, 100+ Free Video Read Alouds
www.indypl.org/blog/for-parents/free-video-read-alouds
"When you are on vacation, running errands or just away from home, read along stories are a great way to fill what can be hours of waiting into a lot of fun." More than a hundred video read alouds are available.

### Reading Rainbow YouTube Channel
www.youtube.com/user/readingrainbow/videos
Visit www.readingrainbow.org for updates on the relaunch of this popular award-winning PBS program.

### Storynory
www.storynory.com
Since 2005, this podcast and website service has been producing free audio stories.

**TRACY SWINTON BAILEY** earned a PhD in Education with a specialization in Language and Literacy at the University of South Carolina in 2013. She began her career as a high school English instructor, and went on to found Freedom Readers, an after school and summer literacy program that was designed and implemented to support families in low-income areas and assist children in achieving their academic goals in reading. She is married to award-winning writer Issac J. Bailey and is the mother of two children.